may

i have

this

dance?

may i have this dance?

a journal through pregnancy

SHEILA HARPER

Copyright 2005 by Sheila Harper
All rights reserved. Written permission must be secured from the publisher to use or reproduce any part of this book, except for brief quotations in critical reviews or articles.

ISBN: 0-9742051-2-5

Cover design by Hope Design
Page design by Mike Towle

Printed in the United States of America
1 2 3 4 5 6 — 09 08 07 06 05

Dedicated to all the women throughout history who, when faced with an unwanted pregnancy, made the courageous choice to parent their child.

Acknowledgments

Thank you first of all, to my Lord and Savior Jesus Christ. Without Him, this book couldn't be written.

Thanks to my two wonderful boys, Jarod and Jakob. Being pregnant with the both of you gave me the insight, inspiration, and motivation needed to write this book. You are two incredible lights in my life. You make me laugh every day. I'm privileged to share my life with you.

Thank you also to Red Haven Cove in Spring City, Tennessee. I enjoyed the solace that place provided me to get in touch with God, and simply write.

How to Use This Book

At the top of each page is what your child might possibly be saying to you if (s)he could talk. These small nuggets are true to a child's development and normal, healthy pregnancy. Next, you will encounter a question that is designed to help you get in touch with your feelings regarding your pregnancy. If on any day the question does not apply to you, then write your own personal thoughts and feelings for that day. At the bottom of the page is a daily takeaway that is inspirational for what you may be going through, thinking, or feeling.

During this crucial time in your life, sometimes you might feel as though there is no one who understands what you're going through. That is where this book comes in. Use it daily to unload your mind, your worries, your doubts, your fears, your joys, and your excitement. If you run out of space, use the blank pages in the back.

This book is designed to carry you through eight months of pregnancy, taking into account you probably found out about your pregnancy thirty days into it. When your child is six months old, pull out this book, start at the beginning, and read all the way through it. You will be blessed!

Blessings on You, Your Pregnancy, and Your Life with Your Child!

Dear Mommy,
I cannot see your face; I don't know your voice; I cannot feel your hands touching me, or your arms holding me. All that is unseen by you is here with me. I know every beat of your heart; for within its music, mine is there, too, sharing the path of love that God is fashioning within your womb.
I am so small . . . a note of music waiting to become part of your life's song; a small raindrop waiting to cry in your ocean of life; a small hollow instrument resting in the silence of your womb, waiting for the Breath of One who will create our song . . . One whose touch awaits my empty ordinary form to be brought into the song-starved world in need of a melody. I am a small wrapped blanket of unconditional love, waiting to be unfolded; a small breeze in a billowing cloud inside you, waiting to share God's creative rainy wonderings when you need to feel washed anew. I am so small . . . the world outside my home sees me not . . . for I am your innocence. I am God's creative thought,
wonderfully woven, formed inside you, by His hand . . . the same hand that will birth my song into the fragments of your life and ask . . .

"May I have this dance?"

Letter written by Angela Klinger

may

i have

this

dance?

A Journal Through Pregnancy

> You might not have been expecting me,
> but I'm no surprise to God!

Day 1 Date: _____

When did you first realize you were pregnant? How did knowing this make you feel?

_____

_____

_____

_____

_____

_____

_____

_____

_____

_____

_____

_____

Daily Takeaway: *"God's ways are as hard to discern as the pathways of the wind, and as mysterious as a tiny baby being formed in a mother's womb."* Ecclesiastes 11:5 NLT.

MAY I HAVE THIS DANCE?

> My heart is beating!

Day 2 Date: _____

Was this pregnancy planned or did it catch you by surprise? Either way, explain your thoughts regarding this pregnancy.

_____

_____

_____

_____

_____

_____

_____

_____

_____

_____

_____

_____

_____

_____

Daily Takeaway: *"Worry is putting question marks where God has put periods."* John R. Rice.

A Journal Through Pregnancy

> God knew me before I was in your tummy!

Day 3   Date: _____

How do you feel about being a mother at this time in your life?

_____

_____

_____

_____

_____

_____

_____

_____

_____

_____

_____

Daily Takeaway: *"Did I conceive a child? Or child, by forming did you conceive a mother?"*
Loving Your Preborn Baby, Carol Van Klompenburg.

MAY I HAVE THIS DANCE?

> Did you know it's already been
> determined whether I'm a boy or a girl?

Day 4 Date: _____

Who have you told about your pregnancy?
How did they react?

_____

_____

_____

_____

_____

_____

_____

_____

_____

_____

Daily Takeaway: *"Do not pray for easy lives. Pray to be strong men and women. Do not pray for tasks equal to your powers but for powers equal to your tasks. Then the doing of your work will be no miracle, but you shall be a miracle. Every day you shall wonder at yourself, at the richness of your life which has come to you by the grace of God."*
Phillips Brooks.

A Journal Through Pregnancy

> My cells are multiplying really quickly.
> They're going to help me grow!

Day 5   Date: _____

Is there anyone you have purposely not told of your pregnancy? Why?

_____

_____

_____

_____

_____

_____

_____

_____

_____

_____

_____

Daily Takeaway: *"God and I together are growing a human, with blood and muscle and bone and brain — a sacred being — someone who bears his own image and who will breathe and cry and eat and have feelings in due time."*
Nine Months and Counting, Alice Chapin.

MAY I HAVE THIS DANCE?

> If you could see me, you
> would see the beginning of my spine!

Day 6 Date: _____

Have you told the father of your child? If so, how has this knowledge changed your relationship with him?

_____

_____

_____

_____

_____

_____

_____

_____

_____

_____

_____

_____

_____

Daily Takeaway: *"Surrender to the unexpected, you can't control it. Things will not always go as planned. Embrace the process."*
Pastor Dan Smith, Cornerstone Church, Nashville, Tennessee.

A Journal Through Pregnancy

> My brain is developing; I'm going to be so smart!

Day 7   Date: _____

Have you told your mother about your pregnancy? How has this knowledge changed that relationship?

_____
_____
_____
_____
_____
_____
_____
_____
_____
_____
_____
_____
_____

Daily Takeaway: *"Wisdom is seeing life from God's point of view."* Bill Gothard.

MAY I HAVE THIS DANCE?

> There is already a place on my head where my eyes are going to be, I can't wait to see you!

Day 8 Date: _____

What anxieties do you have about being pregnant right now?

_____

_____

_____

_____

_____

_____

_____

_____

_____

_____

_____

_____

_____

_____

Daily Takeaway: *"FEAR – False Expectations Appearing Real."* Anonymous.

A Journal Through Pregnancy

> My ears are almost in place. It won't be long and I'll be able to hear you sing to me!

Day 9   Date: _____

What doubts do you have regarding your maternal capabilities?

_____
_____
_____
_____
_____
_____
_____
_____
_____
_____
_____
_____
_____

Daily Takeaway: *"Believe your beliefs and doubt your doubts."* Anonymous.

MAY I HAVE THIS DANCE?

> I can see four different sections of my heart. Wow; this is really neat, Mommy. I wish you could see how fast I'm growing!

Day 10 Date: _____

What kind of grandparents will your child have?

_____
_____
_____
_____
_____
_____
_____
_____
_____
_____
_____
_____
_____

Daily Takeaway: *"Children and grandparents are natural allies."* Anonymous.

A Journal Through Pregnancy

> I have something growing out of both of my sides.
> Those must be my future arms and hands.

Day 11   Date: _____

Have you told the people you work with about your pregnancy? How did they react?

_____
_____
_____
_____
_____
_____
_____
_____
_____
_____
_____
_____
_____

Daily Takeaway: *"Each child is an adventure into a better life, an opportunity to change the old patterns and make it new."*
Hubert H. Humphrey.

MAY I HAVE THIS DANCE?

> I have a cord attached to my stomach.
> That's how you're feeding me!

Day 12　　　　　　　Date: _____

What changes have you already noticed in your body?

_____
_____
_____
_____
_____
_____
_____
_____
_____
_____
_____
_____

Daily Takeaway: *"God has not promised an easy way, but peace at the center of the hard way."* Dale Evans.

A Journal Through Pregnancy

> Thank you, Mommy, for taking such good care of me!

Day 13 Date: _____

What changes have you noticed taking place in your mind?

_____

_____

_____

_____

_____

_____

_____

_____

_____

_____

_____

_____

_____

Daily Takeaway: *"The most important things in life are the thoughts you choose to think."* Marcus Aurelius.

MAY I HAVE THIS DANCE?

> My future legs are sprouting out!

Day 14 Date: _____

What changes in your spirit have you noticed?

_____
_____
_____
_____
_____
_____
_____
_____
_____
_____
_____
_____
_____

○—✦—○

Daily Takeaway: *"As a Mother, my job is to take care of what is possible and trust God with the impossible."* Ruth Bell Graham.

A Journal Through Pregnancy

> My ears are getting into place to hear all the wonderful sounds of our life together!

Day 15 Date: _____

Have you noticed anyone treating you differently? How are they treating you?

_____

_____

_____

_____

_____

_____

_____

_____

_____

_____

_____

_____

Daily Takeaway: *"May the Lord bless you and protect you. May the Lord smile on you and be gracious to you. May the Lord show you His favor and peace."* Numbers 6:24-26 NLT.

MAY I HAVE THIS DANCE?

> I can feel my face starting to form. I hope I look like you!

Day 16   Date: _____

Have you had any good dreams? Write about them.

_____

_____

_____

_____

_____

_____

_____

_____

_____

_____

_____

_____

_____

Daily Takeaway: *"Everything that is done in the world is done by hope."* Martin Luther.

A Journal Through Pregnancy

> My eyes are starting to show color!

Day 17 Date: _____

Have you had any bad dreams? Write about them.

_____

_____

_____

_____

_____

_____

_____

_____

_____

_____

_____

_____

_____

Daily Takeaway: *"While there's life, there's hope."* Cicero.

MAY I HAVE THIS DANCE?

> I have a really big brain. It's already
> working hard to tell me when to breathe.

Day 18 Date: _____

Besides your pregnancy, what major situation do you have going on in your life right now?

_____
_____
_____
_____
_____
_____
_____
_____
_____
_____
_____
_____
_____

Daily Takeaway: *"The peace of God is that eternal calm which lies far too deep in the praying, trusting soul to be reached by any external disturbances."* A. T. Pierson.

A Journal Through Pregnancy

> I have your blood pumping through my veins!

Day 19   Date: _____

Take today off and rest your mind. Don't allow your mind to linger on any doubts, worries, or fears. Just rest.

_____

_____

_____

_____

_____

_____

_____

_____

_____

_____

_____

_____

Daily Takeaway: *"Don't worry about anything. Instead, pray about everything. Tell God what you need, and thank Him for all he has done. If you do this you will experience God's peace, which is far more wonderful than the human mind can understand. His peace will guard your heart and mind as you live in Christ Jesus."* Philippians 4:6-7 NLT.

MAY I HAVE THIS DANCE?

> I can smell things! Did you eat garlic?

Day 20 Date: _____

How has your daily life changed since your pregnancy?

_____
_____
_____
_____
_____
_____
_____
_____
_____
_____
_____
_____

Daily Takeaway: *"Speak with faith about the birth of your baby . . . 'I'm looking forward to the birth of my child within. I know God promises to be with me continually and so I am not afraid. I know God will bless me with calmness and strength.'"* Mari Hanes.

A Journal Through Pregnancy

> My stomach is in place.

Day 21   Date: _____

Who is your doctor or midwife? What are your likes and dislikes about him/her?

_____
_____
_____
_____
_____
_____
_____
_____
_____
_____
_____
_____
_____

○―✦―○

Daily Takeaway: *"Babies are such a nice way to start people."* Don Herold.

MAY I HAVE THIS DANCE?

> I can see my liver!

Day 22   Date: _____

If you listed any dislikes yesterday regarding your doctor or midwife, what can you do to make that part of the relationship more comfortable?

_____
_____
_____
_____
_____
_____
_____
_____
_____
_____
_____
_____

Daily Takeaway: *"You are about to participate in an incredible event, possibly the most profound experience that can happen to a woman. One person becomes two; something too wonderful for words!"* Alice Chapin.

A Journal Through Pregnancy

> My hands are here! I can't wait to throw a ball!

Day 23　　　　　Date: _____

What is your plan to get healthy and stay healthy throughout the pregnancy?

_____

_____

_____

_____

_____

_____

_____

_____

_____

_____

_____

_____

_____

Daily Takeaway: *"We are God's masterpiece. He has created us anew in Christ Jesus."* Ephesians 2:10 NLT.

MAY I HAVE THIS DANCE?

> My forebrain has developed. That's the
> part that will help me understand what
> you are saying to me and experience emotion!

Day 24　　　　　Date: _____

Is there anything in your life or diet that you need to give up? Smoking? Caffeine? If so, what is your plan to get these things out of your life?

_____

_____

_____

_____

_____

_____

_____

_____

_____

_____

_____

_____

_____

_____

Daily Takeaway: *"Habits are the best of servants and the worst of masters."* Anonymous.

A Journal Through Pregnancy

> My midbrain has developed. That's the part that will allow me to hear your beautiful voice!

Day 25　　　　　　　Date: _____

What are the most important values in your life right now?

_____

_____

_____

_____

_____

_____

_____

_____

_____

_____

_____

_____

Daily Takeaway: *"I will meditate on your wonderful miracles."* Psalms 119:27 NLT.

MAY I HAVE THIS DANCE?

> My hindbrain has developed. That's the part that will help me see you that very first time!

Day 26 Date: _____

What are your top four priorities?

___

Daily Takeaway: *"Children are gifts if we accept them."* Kathleen Crilly.

A Journal Through Pregnancy

> My central nervous system is all in place!

Day 27 Date: _____

Name the things that make you the happiest.

_____
_____
_____
_____
_____
_____
_____
_____
_____
_____
_____
_____

Daily Takeaway: *"Sit by yourself today and imagine God at work forming the new life inside you, cell by cell; baby's head, eyes, ears, inner parts, skin, legs, feet. Surely, if we could watch it happening with our eyes, we would fall on our knees at our heavenly Father's feet!"*
Nine Months and Counting, Alice Chapin.

MAY I HAVE THIS DANCE?

> I can see my fingers!

Day 28 Date: _____

Take one thing you named yesterday, write about it, and then go and do it today.

___

Daily Takeaway: *"Whoever is happy will make others happy, too."* Anne Frank.

A Journal Through Pregnancy

> If you could see me, you could pick out my ankles!

Day 29 Date: _____

What is the biggest dream you have for yourself?

_____
_____
_____
_____
_____
_____
_____
_____
_____
_____
_____
_____
_____

Daily Takeaway: *"Not only am I giving birth to a baby, I'm also giving birth to a mother."* **Nine Months and Counting,** Alice Chapin.

> My eyelids are developing!

Day 30 Date: _____

Will the dream you wrote about yesterday change once you have your child? How?

_____
_____
_____
_____
_____
_____
_____
_____
_____
_____
_____
_____

Daily Takeaway: *"You both precede me and follow me. You place your hand of blessing on my head. Such knowledge is too wonderful for me, too great for me to know!"* Psalms 139: 5, 6 NLT.

A Journal Through Pregnancy

> I'm on my way to having more than a million optic nerve fibers in my eyes!

Day 31 Date: _____

What is the most satisfying task you have accomplished in your life?

_____

_____

_____

_____

_____

_____

_____

_____

_____

_____

_____

Daily Takeaway: *"God is the maker of all things. He is the supervisor of this intricate project called pregnancy. I am His partner in growing this brand new life inside. It is almost as if He has borrowed my body for nine months to form this child. Whether I am religious or not, God is there."* **Nine Months and Counting**, Alice Chapin.

MAY I HAVE THIS DANCE?

> God is sculpting my ears.
> One day I may hear crowds cheering for me!

Day 32 Date: _____

Do you believe childbirth will be a satisfying task?

_____
_____
_____
_____
_____
_____
_____
_____
_____
_____
_____
_____
_____

Daily Takeaway: *"The Lord gave me a message. He said, 'I knew you before I formed you in your mother's womb.'"* Jeremiah 1:4, 5 NLT.

A Journal Through Pregnancy

> My blood is moving oxygen
> and food to all parts of my body!

Day 33   Date: _____

What is the main worry in your life right now?

_____

_____

_____

_____

_____

_____

_____

_____

_____

_____

_____

_____

Daily Takeaway: *"Worry is a small trickle of fear that meanders through the mind until it cuts a channel into which all other thoughts are drained."* Anonymous.

MAY I HAVE THIS DANCE?

> You can identify 99 percent of my muscles by now!

Day 34 Date: _____

What steps can you take physically to overcome your main worry?

_____

_____

_____

_____

_____

_____

_____

_____

_____

_____

_____

_____

_____

Daily Takeaway: *"Worry is the interest we pay on tomorrow's troubles."* E. Stanley Jones.

A Journal Through Pregnancy

> My kidneys are working!

Day 35   Date: _____

What mental steps can you take to overcome your main worry?

_____

_____

_____

_____

_____

_____

_____

_____

_____

_____

_____

_____

Daily Takeaway: *"Worry is a destructive process of occupying the mind with thoughts contrary to God's love and care."*
Norman Vincent Peale.

MAY I HAVE THIS DANCE?

> I can see my toes!

Day 36 Date: _____

What are the things you like most about your family?

_____
_____
_____
_____
_____
_____
_____
_____
_____
_____
_____
_____

Daily Takeaway: *"Happiness is not a destination; it is a manner of traveling."* Dr. Haim Ginott.

A Journal Through Pregnancy

> I have cartilage forming between my bones!

Day 37   Date: _____

What things have made you sad lately?

_____
_____
_____
_____
_____
_____
_____
_____
_____
_____
_____
_____
_____

Daily Takeaway: *"The greatest discovery of my generation is that human beings can alter their lives by altering their attitudes of mind."*
William James.

MAY I HAVE THIS DANCE?

> My esophagus is here. I can't wait for you to feed me!

Day 38 Date: _____

Write about three of your best qualities.

_____

_____

_____

_____

_____

_____

_____

_____

_____

_____

_____

_____

_____

_____

Daily Takeaway: *"In quietness and confidence is your strength."* Isaiah 30:15 NLT.

A Journal Through Pregnancy

> My inner ear has developed. That will help me keep my balance. That will come in handy, especially if I become an Olympic athlete!

Day 39 Date: _____

Take today off and rest your mind. Don't allow your mind to linger on any doubts, worries, or fears. Just rest.

Daily Takeaway: *"Don't worry about anything. Instead, pray about everything. Tell God what you need, and thank Him for all He has done. If you do this you will experience God's peace, which is far more wonderful than the human mind can understand. His peace will guard your heart and mind as you live in Christ Jesus."* Philippians 4:6-7 NLT.

MAY I HAVE THIS DANCE?

> Thank you for eating healthy foods.
> You're really helping me to grow!

Day 40 Date: _____

What is one mistake you have made in your life?

_____
_____
_____
_____
_____
_____
_____
_____
_____
_____
_____
_____

Daily Takeaway: *"To confess that you were wrong yesterday is only to acknowledge that you are a little wiser today."* Charles Spurgeon.

A Journal Through Pregnancy

> I can move my body!

Day 41 Date: _____

What have you done about dealing with the mistake you wrote about yesterday?

_____
_____
_____
_____
_____
_____
_____
_____
_____
_____
_____
_____
_____

Daily Takeaway: *"Who doesn't make mistakes? But the greatest error of all is to let any mistake destroy your faith in yourself."*
Norman Vincent Peale.

MAY I HAVE THIS DANCE?

> I had a tail for a long time, but now it's gone. WHEW!

Day 42 Date: _____

What are three changes you need to make because you're about to be a mother?

_____
_____
_____
_____
_____
_____
_____
_____
_____
_____
_____
_____
_____

Daily Takeaway: *"Our life is what our thoughts make it."* Marcus Aurelius.

A Journal Through Pregnancy

> My hands are developing quicker than my feet!

Day 43 Date: _____

What type of woman do you want to become?

_____
_____
_____
_____
_____
_____
_____
_____
_____
_____
_____
_____
_____

○―✦―○

Daily Takeaway: ". . . And Esther obtained favor in the sight of all who saw her." Esther 2:15 NKJV. *Read the story of Esther in your Bible today.* Esther 1:1–9:32.

MAY I HAVE THIS DANCE?

> I just found my knees! I might need
> you to put Band-Aids on them someday.

Day 44 Date: _____

Write about a mother you know that you most admire.

_____
_____
_____
_____
_____
_____
_____
_____
_____
_____
_____
_____
_____

Daily Takeaway: *"Many women who have never thought much about babies at all, or who have never even held a newborn, become excellent mothers. It just works that way. So, take heart."* Alice Chapin.

A Journal Through Pregnancy

> My lips are here. Will you
> teach me how to give you a kiss?

Day 45   Date: _____

Why do you think you will make a good mother? List at least three reasons.

_____
_____
_____
_____
_____
_____
_____
_____
_____
_____
_____
_____
_____

○══▶══○

Daily Takeaway: *"You must conceive it in your heart and mind before you can receive it."* **Your Best Life Now**, Pastor Joel Osteen.

> My lungs are working really well.

Day 46 Date: _____

What are some things you are thankful for?

_____
_____
_____
_____
_____
_____
_____
_____
_____
_____
_____
_____
_____

○━━━○

Daily Takeaway: *"Never lose an opportunity of seeing anything that is beautiful, for beauty is God's handwriting."* Ralph Waldo Emerson. Buy yourself a bundle of fresh flowers today and put them somewhere you will see them and smell them often.

A Journal Through Pregnancy

> My tummy is getting fat!

Day 47 Date: _____

What is something you need to forgive yourself for?

_____

_____

_____

_____

_____

_____

_____

_____

_____

_____

_____

_____

_____

_____

_____

○―✦―○

Daily Takeaway: *"The sin of unforgiveness is a cancer that destroys relationships, eats away at one's own psyche, and worst of all shuts us off from God's grace."* Robert McQuilkin.

MAY I HAVE THIS DANCE?

> This place is so snugly and warm!

Day 48 Date: _____

What steps can you take to forgive yourself for what you wrote about yesterday?

_____
_____
_____
_____
_____
_____
_____
_____
_____
_____
_____
_____
_____
_____

Daily Takeaway: *"Take one step at a time; don't get overwhelmed with the future."* Sheila Harper.

A Journal Through Pregnancy

> My eyelids have completely closed over my eyes. They need protection as they develop and get ready to see you!

Day 49 Date: _____

What is something great that has happened to you in the last seven days?

_____

_____

_____

_____

_____

_____

_____

_____

_____

_____

_____

_____

_____

Daily Takeaway: *"Happiness is not an end in itself. It is a by-product of working, playing, loving, and living."* Dr. Haim Ginott.

MAY I HAVE THIS DANCE?

> I can do so much now!

Day 50 Date: _____

If you have siblings, name a trait you hope your baby will have from each of them.

___

Daily Takeaway: *"God chooses the moms to match the child."* Anonymous.

A Journal Through Pregnancy

> I can kick . . . maybe I'll be a soccer player.

Day 51 Date: _____

Do you have a favorite scripture in the Bible? Write it below. If you don't have one in mind, then look through the Bible and find one that gives you the assurance you need to get through this pregnancy.

_____
_____
_____
_____
_____
_____
_____
_____
_____
_____
_____

Daily Takeaway: *"Belief that divine guidance is real rests upon two foundation facts: First, the reality of God's plan for us; second, the ability of God to communicate with us. On both of these facts the Bible has much to say."* J. I. Packer.

MAY I HAVE THIS DANCE?

> I can curl my toes and turn my feet. . . .
> Maybe I'll be an excellent swimmer.

Day 52 Date: _____

What do you believe is God's purpose for creating this child?

Daily Takeaway: *"When God wants an important thing done in this world or a wrong righted, He doesn't release thunderbolts or stir up earthquakes. He simply has a tiny baby born, perhaps in a very humble home, perhaps of a very humble mother. Then He puts it in the baby's mind, and simply waits. The greatest events of this world are babies."* Edward McDonald.

A Journal Through Pregnancy

> I can make a fist. That will
> come in handy if I learn self-defense.

Day 53 Date: _____

What is one truth you know, for sure, that you can hang onto throughout this pregnancy?

_____

_____

_____

_____

_____

_____

_____

_____

_____

_____

_____

_____

Daily Takeaway: *"All good is gained by those whose thoughts and life are kept pointed to one main thing, not scattered abroad on a thousand."* Stephen McKenna.

MAY I HAVE THIS DANCE?

> I can frown and squint. . . . I just know
> I'm going to make you laugh with all my faces.

Day 54 Date: _____

Who is someone who showed you love this week? How did it make you feel?

___

Daily Takeaway: *"Christ be with me, Christ within me, Christ behind me, Christ before me, Christ to comfort me and restore me. Christ beneath me, Christ above me, Christ in hearts of all who love me, Christ in mouth of friend or stranger."* Saint Patrick.

A Journal Through Pregnancy

> From what I can see in here,
> your body is changing a lot, Mommy!

Day 55 Date: _____

Who is someone you have shown love to this week? How did it make you feel?

_____

_____

_____

_____

_____

_____

_____

_____

_____

_____

_____

_____

_____

Daily Takeaway: *"A Blessing is not a blessing until it is spoken."*
Your Best Life Now, Pastor Joel Osteen.

MAY I HAVE THIS DANCE?

> My fingernails and toenails are here!

Day 56   Date: _____

What dreams do you have for your child?

_____

_____

_____

_____

_____

_____

_____

_____

_____

_____

_____

_____

Daily Takeaway: *"When a child is born into the world, God draws His hand out from near His own heart and lends something of Himself to the parent and says, 'Keep it till I come.'"* Henry Ward Beecher.

A Journal Through Pregnancy

> My rib cage is closing.
> That will protect all my inside stuff.

Day 57   Date: _____

Write more about the dreams you have for your child.

_____

_____

_____

_____

_____

_____

_____

_____

_____

_____

Daily Takeaway: *"Always be the best parent you can be. Remember what you plant now, you will harvest later."* Og Mandino.
Remember this: "A farmer who plants only a few seeds will get a small crop. But the one who plants generously will get a generous crop." II Corinthians 9:6 **NLT**.

MAY I HAVE THIS DANCE?

> Just in the last few weeks I have doubled my size! I'm working hard to grow strong.

Day 58 Date: _____

Write out a prayer to God for your unborn child.

_____

_____

_____

_____

_____

_____

_____

_____

_____

_____

_____

_____

_____

Daily Takeaway: *"Prayer delights God's ear, it melts His heart, and it opens His hand; God cannot deny a praying soul."* Thomas Watson.

A Journal Through Pregnancy

> If you could touch me, I would feel it.

Day 59 Date: _____

Take today off and rest your mind. Don't allow your mind to linger on any doubts, worries, or fears. Just rest.

_____

_____

_____

_____

_____

_____

_____

_____

_____

_____

_____

Daily Takeaway: *"Don't worry about anything. Instead, pray about everything. Tell God what you need, and thank Him for all He has done. If you do this, you will experience God's peace, which is far more wonderful than the human mind can understand. His peace will guard your heart and mind as you live in Christ Jesus."*
Philippians 4:6-7 NLT.

MAY I HAVE THIS DANCE?

> My intestines are in place.

Day 60 Date: _____

Think about what your life will be like in ten years. What do you see?

_____

_____

_____

_____

_____

_____

_____

_____

_____

_____

_____

Daily Takeaway: *"Find a place where people will encourage you and challenge you to be the best you can be. Find a place where people inspire you to reach for new heights. Friend, you have to envision good things happening to you before they ever will."*
Your Best Life Now, Pastor Joel Osteen.

A Journal Through Pregnancy

> My jaws are getting hard.
> I'll need those to talk to you.

Day 61 Date: _____

Has anyone shared an old wives' tale about pregnancy with you? What did you think about it?

___

Daily Takeaway: *"God is the friend of silence. See how nature, trees, flowers, and grass grow in silence? The more we receive in silent prayer, the more we can give in our active life."* Mother Teresa.

MAY I HAVE THIS DANCE?

> I hope you're drinking lots of milk because my teeth and bones are really growing.

Day 62 Date: _____

In what ways do you think being a mother will change you?

_____
_____
_____
_____
_____
_____
_____
_____
_____
_____
_____
_____

Daily Takeaway: *"The hand that rocks the cradle rules the nation and its destiny."* South African Proverb.

A Journal Through Pregnancy

> I can suck my thumb!

Day 63 Date: _____

If you have other children, how have they reacted to this pregnancy?

_____

_____

_____

_____

_____

_____

_____

_____

_____

_____

_____

_____

Daily Takeaway: *"People are what their mothers make them."* Ralph Waldo Emerson.

MAY I HAVE THIS DANCE?

> I don't have any more organs that
> need to be created. They're all here!

Day 64 Date: _____

How did your children's reaction to this pregnancy affect you?

_____

_____

_____

_____

_____

_____

_____

_____

_____

_____

_____

_____

_____

○━━○

Daily Takeaway: *"Bless the Lord who is my rock. He gives me strength. He is my loving ally . . . my deliverer."* Psalm 144:1, 2 NLT.

A Journal Through Pregnancy

> All we have to do over the next few
> months is for you to eat healthy food,
> and I'll grow. We make a good team, Mommy!

Day 65 Date: _____

How is this pregnancy different from what you thought it would be?

_____

_____

_____

_____

_____

_____

_____

_____

_____

_____

_____

Daily Takeaway: *"What parts of your life seem to be on hold right now? Do you understand that this may be part of God's plan for you? The Bible has more than enough clear direction to keep us busy while we're waiting for some particular part of life to move ahead."*
Life Application Bible, "Sarah" sketch in Genesis 18.

MAY I HAVE THIS DANCE?

> I never knew how handy these thumbs could be!

Day 66 Date: _____

Have you had any weird dreams? Write about them.

_____
_____
_____
_____
_____
_____
_____
_____
_____
_____
_____

Daily Takeaway: *"The human soul is God's treasury, out of which He coins unspeakable riches, thoughts and feelings, desires and yearning, faith and hope. These are the most precious things which God finds in us."* Henry Ward Beecher.

A Journal Through Pregnancy

> I am unique. No one has
> ever been created quite like me!

Day 67 Date: _____

Are there times you worry? Write about these times.

Daily Takeaway: *"When you are tempted to fret and worry, divert yourself. Don't sit around with the curtains drawn, wringing your hands. Throw open the windows, find something that needs to be done, and get busy."* Unknown.

MAY I HAVE THIS DANCE?

> My feet are ready to walk and run!

Day 68 Date: _____

What are the things you worry about?

_____

_____

_____

_____

_____

_____

_____

_____

_____

_____

_____

Daily Takeaway: The phrase "*Be not afraid*" is found more than three hundred times in the New Testament. Jesus said, "Do not worry about tomorrow, for tomorrow will worry about its own things." Matthew 6:3, 4 **NKJV**.

A Journal Through Pregnancy

> My heart looks just like yours, only smaller.

Day 69 Date: _____

What do you believe is the antidote for worry?

_____
_____
_____
_____
_____
_____
_____
_____
_____
_____
_____

Daily Takeaway: *"The Lord is my shepherd, I have everything I need; He lets me rest in green meadows; He leads me beside peaceful streams; He renews my strength; He guides me along right paths, bringing honor to His name."* Psalm 23:1-3 NLT.

MAY I HAVE THIS DANCE?

> I can turn my head!

Day 70   Date: _____

How do you think worrying affects your unborn child?

_____
_____
_____
_____
_____
_____
_____
_____
_____
_____
_____

Daily Takeaway: *"What are you allowing your mind to dwell on? Are you focused on your problems? Are you constantly dwelling on negative things? How you view life makes all the difference in the world."*
Your Best Life Now, Joel Osteen.

A Journal Through Pregnancy

> I'm moving all over the place
> in here, but you can't feel me.

Day 71 Date: _____

What steps can you take to stop worrying?

_____
_____
_____
_____
_____
_____
_____
_____
_____
_____
_____
_____
_____

Daily Takeaway: *"It's time to think about what you're thinking about."* **Your Best Life Now**, Pastor Joel Osteen.

MAY I HAVE THIS DANCE?

> My fingerprints are here. No one else ever had the same fingerprints as mine.

Day 72 Date: _____

How do you picture God?

_____

_____

_____

_____

_____

_____

_____

_____

_____

Daily Takeaway: *"Did you know that God is your protector, provider, hope, healer, father, and strength? He is able to see all that happens to you. He is able to calm any storm in your life. He is able to be there even when your friends and family aren't. He is able to give you a destiny. He is able to plan your future. He is able to open every door to get you to that future. He is able to put you back on the right path, even when you've chosen the wrong one. He is able to forgive you of your sins. He is able to send His very Son to die for you in order for that to happen. He is able to love you more than anyone on this earth has the capability to love. He is able to save your soul."* **SaveOne—A Guide to Emotional Healing after Abortion**, Sheila Harper.

A Journal Through Pregnancy

> I know whether I'm a boy
> or girl, BUT I'M NOT TELLING!

Day 73 Date: _____

How do you think God pictures you?

___

Daily Takeaway: *"Constantly remind yourself that you are made in the image of Almighty God. Remind yourself that He has crowned you with glory and honor, that you are God's own masterpiece."*
Your Best Life Now, Pastor Joel Osteen.

MAY I HAVE THIS DANCE?

> All my private parts are here.
> I'm sure you will tell me what to do with those!

Day 74 Date: _____

How do you picture yourself?

_____
_____
_____
_____
_____
_____
_____
_____
_____
_____
_____
_____
_____

Daily Takeaway: *"You will never rise above the image you have of yourself in your own mind."*
Your Best Life Now, Pastor Joel Osteen.

A Journal Through Pregnancy

> My eyes have been really far apart,
> but now they're moving much closer together.

Day 75 Date: _____

Do you believe you were fair yesterday when you wrote about yourself? Why or why not?

_____

_____

_____

_____

_____

_____

_____

_____

_____

_____

_____

_____

_____

Daily Takeaway: *"The mind of man is the battleground on which every moral and spiritual battle is fought."* J. Oswald Sanders.

MAY I HAVE THIS DANCE?

> Mommy . . . I love you.

Day 76 Date: _____

What dreams do you have academically for your child?

_____
_____
_____
_____
_____
_____
_____
_____
_____
_____
_____
_____
_____

Daily Takeaway: *"Instill respect for authority in your children by modeling that behavior. To send kids the right messages, establish consequences for moral lapses, and follow through."* Dr. Laura Schlessinger.

A Journal Through Pregnancy

> I'm getting stronger with each passing day!

Day 77   Date: _____

What dreams do you have for your child regarding family?

_____

_____

_____

_____

_____

_____

_____

_____

_____

_____

_____

_____

_____

Daily Takeaway: *"All that I am or hope to be I owe to my mother."* Abraham Lincoln.

MAY I HAVE THIS DANCE?

> My ears look more like your ears now.

Day 78 Date: _____

What dreams do you have spiritually for your child?

_____
_____
_____
_____
_____
_____
_____
_____
_____
_____
_____
_____

Daily Takeaway: *"I talk, and talk, and talk, and I haven't taught people in fifty years what my father taught by example in one week."* Mario Cuomo, former New York governor.

A Journal Through Pregnancy

> My heart is beating really fast! I can't wait until the first time you get to hear it, too.

Day 79 Date: _____

Take today off and rest your mind. Don't allow your mind to linger on any doubts, worries, or fears. Just rest.

_____
_____
_____
_____
_____
_____
_____
_____
_____
_____
_____
_____

Daily Takeaway: *"Don't worry about anything. Instead, pray about everything. Tell God what you need, and thank Him for all He has done. If you do this you will experience God's peace, which is far more wonderful than the human mind can understand. His peace will guard your heart and mind as you live in Christ Jesus."* Philippians 4:6-7 NLT.

MAY I HAVE THIS DANCE?

> My eyes are still closed.
> God must be working really hard on them!

Day 80 Date: _____

Do you believe you are courageous? Why or why not?

_____

_____

_____

_____

_____

_____

_____

_____

_____

_____

_____

_____

Daily Takeaway: *"The definition of courage: Grace under pressure."* Ernest Hemingway.

A Journal Through Pregnancy

> My arms and legs are looking really good!

Day 81 Date: _____

Have you had to deal with any criticism during your pregnancy? Write about it.

Daily Takeaway: *"They're saying things that are not true; O blessed Lord, what shall I do? He answers, 'What is that to thee? Thy duty is to follow me.'"* Anonymous.

MAY I HAVE THIS DANCE?

> I can't wait to wrap my arms
> around your neck and give you a big hug!

Day 82 Date: _____

Do you feel anger toward anyone involved with this pregnancy? Who and why?

___

Daily Takeaway: *"Stop your anger, turn from your rage, do not envy others; it only leads to harm."* Psalm 37:8 NLT.

A Journal Through Pregnancy

> During this month my weight is going to quadruple!

Day 83 Date: _____

If you are holding onto anger or unforgiveness towards another person, how do you think this affects you? How does it affect your pregnancy?

_____
_____
_____
_____
_____
_____
_____
_____
_____
_____
_____
_____

Daily Takeaway: *"Anger is an acid that can do more harm to the vessel in which it is stored than to anything on which it is poured."*
The Baptist Beacon.

MAY I HAVE THIS DANCE?

> My body keeps jumping. I think I have hiccups!

Day 84 Date: _____

What is your biggest fear concerning this pregnancy?

_____
_____
_____
_____
_____
_____
_____
_____
_____
_____
_____
_____

Daily Takeaway: *"When a man is defeated by life, it is always due ultimately to the fact that he is suffering from a spirit of fear. The spirit of fear is the real, the ultimate cause of all failure in life and of all unhappiness."* Dr. Martin Lloyd Jones.

A Journal Through Pregnancy

> My ears are in their final position.

Day 85 Date: _____

What is your greatest joy concerning this pregnancy?

_____
_____
_____
_____
_____
_____
_____
_____
_____
_____
_____
_____
_____

Daily Takeaway: *"Happiness is an emotion and joy is an attitude. Emotions come and go, but attitudes come and grow."*
Pastor Robert J. Morgan.

MAY I HAVE THIS DANCE?

> My bones are hardening. I'm going to be so strong!

Day 86　　　　　　　Date: _____

What are you anticipating the most regarding this pregnancy?

___

Daily Takeaway: *"Focusing on the largeness of my pregnancy rather than on my large size, the huge miracle of it all, the majesty of creation and my baby's potential, helped me enjoy my convex shape."*
Alice Chapin.

A Journal Through Pregnancy

> If you could hold me, your palm would cradle me.

Day 87 Date: _____

If this is not your first pregnancy, what is different this time?

_____
_____
_____
_____
_____
_____
_____
_____
_____
_____
_____
_____
_____

Daily Takeaway: *"Keep vigilant watch over your heart; that's where life starts."* Proverbs 4:23, The Message Bible.

MAY I HAVE THIS DANCE?

> My heart is pumping 25 quarts of blood per day!

Day 88   Date: _____

How do you feel about your weight gain?

_____
_____
_____
_____
_____
_____
_____
_____
_____
_____
_____
_____
_____

Daily Takeaway: *"A glad heart makes a happy face."* Proverbs 15:13 NLT.

A Journal Through Pregnancy

> My reflexes are developing.

Day 89　　　　　　　　Date: _____

What do you think about how your body is changing?

_____

_____

_____

_____

_____

_____

_____

_____

_____

_____

_____

_____

Daily Takeaway: *"God does not grow tired. When your energy runs out, when weariness sets in, go back to Him anytime day or night and claim His strength. God created your body. He knows well how to recreate it with strength and vitality."*
Nine Months and Counting, Alice Chapin.

MAY I HAVE THIS DANCE?

> By the time I'm born, I'll have more than 70 reflexes!

Day 90   Date: _____

Will you continue to work once the baby is born?
Why or why not?

_____

_____

_____

_____

_____

_____

_____

_____

_____

_____

_____

_____

_____

Daily Takeaway: *"Never lose an opportunity of seeing anything that is beautiful, for beauty is God's handwriting."* Ralph Waldo Emerson.

A Journal Through Pregnancy

> **If you could see me, you would be able to see through my skin.**

Day 91   Date: _____

Describe what you think your child's personality will be like.

_____

_____

_____

_____

_____

_____

_____

_____

_____

_____

_____

_____

Daily Takeaway: *"It is my firm belief that approximately 85 percent of one's adult personality is formed by the time he is six years old. Those first six years, therefore, are obviously the most crucial."*
Christian Child-rearing and Personal Development, Paul Meier.

MAY I HAVE THIS DANCE?

> I'm starting to grow hair on my head!

Day 92 Date: _____

Who has been your greatest source of encouragement throughout this pregnancy?

_____
_____
_____
_____
_____
_____
_____
_____
_____
_____
_____
_____

○—✦—○

Daily Takeaway: *"Find the good and applaud."* Zig Ziglar.

A Journal Through Pregnancy

> If you had an ultrasound, you would find out if I am a boy or a girl!

Day 93 Date: _____

Write a prayer to God for the person you wrote about yesterday.

___

Daily Takeaway: *"Prayer is a mighty instrument, not for getting man's will done in Heaven, but for getting God's will done on earth."* Robert Law.

MAY I HAVE THIS DANCE?

> If I'm a girl, I already have all the eggs in my ovaries that I will have for the rest of my life.

Day 94   Date: _____

Name three things that make you happy.

_____

_____

_____

_____

_____

_____

_____

_____

_____

_____

_____

_____

_____

Daily Takeaway: *"Happiness is a habit."* Anonymous.

A Journal Through Pregnancy

| My legs and arms are really long! |

Day 95 Date: _____

Have you felt lonely during any part of this pregnancy? Explain.

_____
_____
_____
_____
_____
_____
_____
_____
_____
_____
_____
_____
_____
_____

Daily Takeaway: *"Loneliness becomes our 'friend' when it forces us to enjoy the friendship of God as we would the friendship of others."* Bill Gothard.

MAY I HAVE THIS DANCE?

> Have you felt me yet? I'm trying to get your attention!

Day 96 Date: _____

Are you going to find out the sex of your child? Why or why not?

Daily Takeaway: *"You made all the delicate inner parts of my body and knit me together in my mother's womb. You saw me before I was born. Every day of my life was recorded in your book. Every moment was laid out."* Psalm 139:13, 16 NLT.

A Journal Through Pregnancy

> Mommy . . . thank you for making such a warm, cozy place for me to grow and get ready to live life!

Day 97   Date: _____

What do you think about having a boy?

_____
_____
_____
_____
_____
_____
_____
_____
_____
_____
_____
_____
_____

Daily Takeaway: *"I created you and have cared for you since before you were born. I will be your God throughout your lifetime. . . . I made you, and I will care for you. I will carry you along."* Isaiah 46:3, 4 NLT.

MAY I HAVE THIS DANCE?

> I have been curled over, but
> now I'm growing taller and straighter.

Day 98 Date: _____

What do you think about having a girl?

___

Daily Takeaway: *"You both precede and follow me. You place your hand of blessing on my head. Such knowledge is too wonderful for me, too great for me to know."* Psalm 139:5, 6 NLT.

A Journal Through Pregnancy

> My vocal cords are here. I'll really get to use those in a few short months!

Day 99 Date: _____

Take today off and rest your mind. Don't allow your mind to linger on any doubts, worries, or fears. Just rest.

_____
_____
_____
_____
_____
_____
_____
_____
_____
_____
_____
_____

Daily Takeaway: *"Don't worry about anything. Instead, pray about everything. Tell God what you need, and thank Him for all He has done. If you do this you will experience God's peace, which is far more wonderful than the human mind can understand. His peace will guard your heart and mind as you live in Christ Jesus."* Philippians 4:6-7 NLT.

MAY I HAVE THIS DANCE?

I CAN HEAR YOUR VOICE!!!

Day 100 Date: _____

Have you been thinking of names for your child? Write about the ones you like.

_____
_____
_____
_____
_____
_____
_____
_____
_____
_____
_____
_____
_____

Daily Takeaway: *"The entry of a child into any situation changes the whole situation."* I. Murdoch.

A Journal Through Pregnancy

> You have a beautiful voice, Mommy!

Day 101   Date: _____

What are some of the food cravings you have had?

_____

_____

_____

_____

_____

_____

_____

_____

_____

_____

_____

_____

_____

Daily Takeaway: *"The body is matter; but it is God's creation. When it is neglected or scoffed at, God himself is insulted."* Michael Quoist.

MAY I HAVE THIS DANCE?

> I could listen to you talk nonstop. I love your voice!

Day 102 Date: _____

What is your attitude toward food right now?

___

Daily Takeaway: *"Birth is the sudden opening of a window through which you look out upon a stupendous prospect. For what has happened? A miracle. You have exchanged nothing for the possibility of everything."* William MacNeile Dixon.

A Journal Through Pregnancy

> Please sing me a song!

Day 103   Date: _____

Have you had any conflicting feelings about motherhood?

_____
_____
_____
_____
_____
_____
_____
_____
_____
_____
_____
_____
_____
_____

Daily Takeaway: *"Let God do it His way."*
Your Best Life Now, Pastor Joel Osteen.

MAY I HAVE THIS DANCE?

> I've been testing my reflexes; can you feel it?

Day 104 Date: _____

Are you having any thoughts that are making you feel guilty? Write about them.

Daily Takeaway: *"Our defeat or victory begins with what we think, and if we guard our thoughts we shall not have much trouble anywhere else along the line."* Vince Havner.

A Journal Through Pregnancy

> Almost all my muscles have developed!

Day 105 Date: _____

How do you think guilty feelings might affect your pregnancy?

_____
_____
_____
_____
_____
_____
_____
_____
_____
_____
_____
_____
_____
_____

Daily Takeaway: *"You can't take your failures and let them determine who you are. Identity isn't based on failure but on Jesus Christ."* Pastor Maury Davis, Cornerstone Church.

MAY I HAVE THIS DANCE?

> I like to sleep a lot in here. Sleeping helps me grow.

Day 106　　　　　　　Date: _____

What do you believe is the remedy for feeling guilty?

_____
_____
_____
_____
_____
_____
_____
_____
_____
_____
_____

Daily Takeaway: *"We use God's mighty weapons, not mere worldly weapons, to knock down the Devil's strongholds. With these weapons, we break down every proud argument that keeps people from knowing God. With these weapons, we conquer their rebellious ideas, and we teach them to obey Christ."* II Corinthians 10:4, 5 NLT.

A Journal Through Pregnancy

> I just turned a somersault. This is fun!

Day 107   Date: _____

Have you felt the baby move? If so, how did it make you feel?

_____

_____

_____

_____

_____

_____

_____

_____

_____

_____

_____

_____

Daily Takeaway: *"Birth, one final push and you burst forth wet and waiting, your farewell to womb and your hello to world. Love's labor done, I gaze . . . awed to silence."*
Loving Your Preborn Baby, Carol Van Klompenburg.

MAY I HAVE THIS DANCE?

> Have you heard my beating heart?

Day 108 Date: _____

How did you picture your child the first time you felt the movement?

_____

_____

_____

_____

_____

_____

_____

_____

_____

_____

_____

_____

Daily Takeaway: *"Baby, are you as anxious to come forth from the crowded womb as I am to have it happen? Maybe we are both counting the days."* **Nine Months and Counting**, Alice Chapin.

A Journal Through Pregnancy

> My legs are the size they
> will be the first time you see me!

Day 109　　　　　　　Date: _____

Do you want your child to be good at sports? Musically inclined?

_____

_____

_____

_____

_____

_____

_____

_____

_____

_____

_____

_____

_____

Daily Takeaway: *"Everything is possible for him who believes."* Mark 9:23 NIV.

MAY I HAVE THIS DANCE?

> If you could see me, you would think
> I looked just like a sleeping newborn baby.

Day 110 Date: _____

Has being pregnant brought back thoughts of your own childhood?

___

Daily Takeaway: *"God made you, and He has programmed you for victory."* **Your Best Life Now**, Pastor Joel Osteen.

A Journal Through Pregnancy

> I have eyelashes!

Day 111 Date: _____

Did you have a good or difficult childhood?

_____
_____
_____
_____
_____
_____
_____
_____
_____
_____
_____
_____
_____

Daily Takeaway: *"I've come to change everything, turn everything right side up."* Luke 12:50, The Message Bible.

MAY I HAVE THIS DANCE?

> All my organs are working,
> but I still can't live without you!

Day 112 Date: _____

What are two of the greatest events that happened to you as a child?

_____
_____
_____
_____
_____
_____
_____
_____
_____
_____
_____
_____
_____
_____

Daily Takeaway: *"A happy family is but an earlier heaven."* Anonymous.

A Journal Through Pregnancy

> My circulation is working perfectly!

Day 113   Date: _____

What are two of the worst events that happened to you as a child?

_____
_____
_____
_____
_____
_____
_____
_____
_____
_____
_____
_____

○─→─○

Daily Takeaway: *"You may have deep scars from emotional wounds, but don't let your past determine your future. You can't do anything about what's happened to you, but you can choose how you will face what's in front of you."* **Your Best Life Now**, Pastor Joel Osteen.

MAY I HAVE THIS DANCE?

> My brain is producing 100,000
> new cells per minute. I'll have more
> than 100 billion by the time I get to see you!

Day 114   Date: _____

What events from your childhood do you want to bring forward into this child's life?

_____
_____
_____
_____
_____
_____
_____
_____
_____
_____
_____
_____

Daily Takeaway: *"The fundamental fact of existence is that this trust in God, this faith, is the firm foundation under everything that makes life worth living. It's our handle on what we can't see."*
Hebrews 11:1, The Message Bible.

A Journal Through Pregnancy

> Have you thought of my name?
> If so, I would really like to hear it.

Day 115　　　　　　Date: _____

What is your plan to make what you wrote about yesterday happen?

_____

_____

_____

_____

_____

_____

_____

_____

_____

_____

Daily Takeaway: *"There is a time for everything, a season for every activity under heaven. A time to be born and a time to die; A time to plant and a time to harvest; A time to cry and a time to laugh; A time to grieve and a time to dance."* Ecclesiastes 3:1-2, 4 NLT.

MAY I HAVE THIS DANCE?

> I'm half the length I'll be when I'm born!

Day 116 Date: _____

What events from your childhood do you want to make sure never affect your child?

___

Daily Takeaway: *"Learn to speak God's favor over every area of your life."* **Your Best Life Now**, Pastor Joel Osteen.

A Journal Through Pregnancy

> I have eyebrows and hair on my head, but it's all white. It will eventually change colors and look more like yours!

Day 117 Date: _____

What is your plan to make happen what you wrote about yesterday?

_____

_____

_____

_____

_____

_____

_____

_____

_____

_____

_____

_____

Daily Takeaway: *"How can we find the calm and quiet we need to be truly content? By seeking for and immersing ourselves in God."*
In Pursuit of Peace, Joyce Meyer.

MAY I HAVE THIS DANCE?

> I'm really skinny right now, but by the time I'm born, I'll be cuddly and fat!

Day 118   Date: _____

If you could have any future you wanted, what would it hold?

_____
_____
_____
_____
_____
_____
_____
_____
_____
_____
_____
_____
_____

Daily Takeaway: *"Happiness is a decision you make, not an emotion you feel."* **Your Best Life Now**, Pastor Joel Osteen.

A Journal Through Pregnancy

> I can hold onto stuff. I'm getting stronger!

Day 119 Date: _____

Take today off and rest your mind. Don't allow your mind to linger on any doubts, worries, or fears. Just rest.

_____
_____
_____
_____
_____
_____
_____
_____
_____
_____
_____
_____

○─✦─○

Daily Takeaway: *"Don't worry about anything. Instead, pray about everything. Tell God what you need, and thank Him for all He has done. If you do this you will experience God's peace, which is far more wonderful than the human mind can understand. His peace will guard your heart and mind as you live in Christ Jesus."* Philippians 4:6-7 NLT.

MAY I HAVE THIS DANCE?

> My body is finally catching up with my big head!

Day 120 Date: _____

Take your time today and write a letter to your child.

_____
_____
_____
_____
_____
_____
_____
_____
_____
_____
_____
_____
_____
_____

Daily Takeaway: *"Wisdom is seeing life from God's point of view."* Bill Gothard.

A Journal Through Pregnancy

> Mommy, I love you more and more every day!

Day 121 Date: _____

Does being in the hospital bring about any negative thoughts or feelings?

_____

_____

_____

_____

_____

_____

_____

_____

_____

_____

_____

_____

_____

Daily Takeaway: *"Come to me, all of you who are weary and carry heavy burdens, and I will give you rest."* Matthew 11:28 NLT.

MAY I HAVE THIS DANCE?

> You sure have been eating some
> good food lately. Keep it coming!

Day 122 Date: _____

What do you think the hospital stay will be like?

_____
_____
_____
_____
_____
_____
_____
_____
_____
_____
_____
_____
_____

Daily Takeaway: *"Reflect upon your present blessings, of which every man has many; not on your past misfortunes, of which all men have some."* Charles Dickens.

A Journal Through Pregnancy

> My lungs are in place, but they're still developing.

Day 123   Date: _____

Do you have feelings of love for your child yet?

_____

_____

_____

_____

_____

_____

_____

_____

_____

_____

_____

_____

_____

Daily Takeaway: *"I love those little people, and it is not a slight thing, when they so fresh from God love us."* Charles Dickens.

MAY I HAVE THIS DANCE?

> I'm making blinking movements with my eyes.
> Before long my eyes will be opened again!

Day 124   Date: _____

Do you feel as though you are creating a bond with your child yet?

_____

_____

_____

_____

_____

_____

_____

_____

_____

_____

_____

_____

_____

Daily Takeaway: *"Pray above all things for a strong faith active in love."* **Ten Rules for Living**, Pastor Heinrich Bellinger.

A Journal Through Pregnancy

> I'm getting a little bit crowded in here!

Day 125   Date: _____

Is there anything that you do or eat that evokes a reaction from your child?

_____

_____

_____

_____

_____

_____

_____

_____

_____

_____

_____

Daily Takeaway: *"Sometimes the journey into motherhood seems so amazing, so astounding, that it doesn't seem real – feels more like fiction – because all of these incredible events are going on in a perfectly ordered way in my deepest and most intimate private parts where no one can see, not even me."* **Nine Months and Counting**, Alice Chapin.

MAY I HAVE THIS DANCE?

> My skin is all wrinkly, making room for fat!

Day 126 Date: _____

How do you feel about being the number-one source for everything in your child's life?

_____
_____
_____
_____
_____
_____
_____
_____
_____
_____
_____

Daily Takeaway: *"Lord, how can this be? A real person inside me! A child that will have to come out! This new life actually takes up space and is growing hour by hour, with new cells, new blood, new muscle, new skin, hair, and bone — all of those marvelous increases coming out of nowhere to enhance my baby's size."*
Nine Months and Counting, Alice Chapin.

A Journal Through Pregnancy

> If you could see me, you would still be able to see through my skin!

Day 127   Date: _____

How will you be more responsible once your child is here?

_____

_____

_____

_____

_____

_____

_____

_____

_____

_____

_____

_____

_____

Daily Takeaway: *"It is not enough to have a good mind; the main thing is to use it well."* Descartes.

MAY I HAVE THIS DANCE?

> I'm going to gain another half-pound this week!

Day 128　　　　　　Date: _____

How will you be more organized once your child is here?

_____
_____
_____
_____
_____
_____
_____
_____
_____
_____
_____
_____

Daily Takeaway: *"Our life is what our thoughts make it."*
Marcus Aurelius.

A Journal Through Pregnancy

> Most of the weight I'm gaining is from my growing muscles!

Day 129 Date: _____

How will you change the way you handle money once your child is here?

_____

_____

_____

_____

_____

_____

_____

_____

_____

_____

_____

_____

_____

_____

_____

Daily Takeaway: *"When your outgo exceeds your income, your upkeep will be your downfall."* Anonymous.

MAY I HAVE THIS DANCE?

> I'm really getting to know you. I can hear your heart beat!

Day 130 Date: _____

What do you believe about prayer?

_____
_____
_____
_____
_____
_____
_____
_____
_____
_____
_____
_____
_____

Daily Takeaway: *"A day hemmed in prayer is less likely to come unraveled."* Anonymous.

A Journal Through Pregnancy

> I can hear your stomach growling. You must be hungry a lot!

Day 131   Date: _____

What do you believe about faith?

_____
_____
_____
_____
_____
_____
_____
_____
_____
_____
_____
_____
_____
_____

Daily Takeaway: *"Little faith will bring your soul to heaven, but great faith will bring heaven to your soul."* Anonymous.

MAY I HAVE THIS DANCE?

> I can actually hear you breathing!

Day 132 Date: _____

What do you believe about God's Grace?

_____

_____

_____

_____

_____

_____

_____

_____

_____

_____

_____

_____

Daily Takeaway: *"God's Empowering Presence."*
Definition of grace, by John Bevere.

A Journal Through Pregnancy

> I'm producing white blood cells.
> These will help me stay healthy!

Day 133 Date: _____

If you are single, what are your feelings on marriage?
If you are married, what is your marriage like?

_____

_____

_____

_____

_____

_____

_____

_____

_____

_____

_____

Daily Takeaway: *"The ever-loving Christ is here to bless you. The nearer you keep Him, the nearer you will be to one another."*
Geoffrey Francis Fisher, the archbishop of Canterbury, at the wedding of Queen Elizabeth II.

I have a tongue!

Day 134 Date: _____

What wisdom have you gained throughout this pregnancy?

_____
_____
_____
_____
_____
_____
_____
_____
_____
_____
_____
_____
_____
_____

Daily Takeaway: *"Wisdom is seeing life from God's point of view."* Bill Gothard.

A Journal Through Pregnancy

> My skin is changing colors. You can't see through me any longer!

Day 135 Date: _____

How can you apply the wisdom you wrote about yesterday?

_____
_____
_____
_____
_____
_____
_____
_____
_____
_____
_____
_____
_____

Daily Takeaway: *"Wisdom is the ability to apply biblical truths to all life situations."* Anonymous.

MAY I HAVE THIS DANCE?

> I've been sucking my thumb. I really enjoy it!

Day 136 Date: _____

Do you believe you can trust God? Why or why not?

_____
_____
_____
_____
_____
_____
_____
_____
_____
_____
_____
_____
_____

Daily Takeaway: *"God usually meets us at our level of expectancy."* **Your Best Life Now**, Pastor Joel Osteen.

A Journal Through Pregnancy

> My nostrils are opening. I have a cute nose!

Day 137 Date: _____

What is the best thing about your home life right now?

___

Daily Takeaway: *"Choose to delight in the gifts God has already given you. Enjoy the simple things in life; sunsets, delicious food, loving friends and family, beautiful flowers, and peaceful pleasures."*
101 Ways to Relax and Reduce Stress, Candy Paull.

MAY I HAVE THIS DANCE?

> I have 150 joints in my spine!

Day 138　　　　　Date: _____

What is the most difficult thing about your home life right now?

_____
_____
_____
_____
_____
_____
_____
_____
_____
_____
_____
_____
_____

Daily Takeaway: *"Smooth seas do not make skillful sailors."* African Proverb.

A Journal Through Pregnancy

> I'm trying to breathe on my own.
> I'm trying to make you proud of me!

Day 139 Date: _____

Take today off and rest your mind. Don't allow your mind to linger on any doubts, worries, or fears. Just rest.

_____

_____

_____

_____

_____

_____

_____

_____

_____

_____

_____

_____

○━━✦━━○

Daily Takeaway: *"Don't worry about anything. Instead, pray about everything. Tell God what you need, and thank Him for all He has done. If you do this you will experience God's peace, which is far more wonderful than the human mind can understand. His peace will guard your heart and mind as you live in Christ Jesus."* Philippians 4:6-7 NLT.

MAY I HAVE THIS DANCE?

> There is a lot of stuff
> happening with my lungs this week!

Day 140   Date: _____

How is the relationship between you and your doctor or midwife?

_____
_____
_____
_____
_____
_____
_____
_____
_____
_____
_____
_____
_____
_____

Daily Takeaway: *"Prayer bathes the soul in an atmosphere of the divine presence."* Charles Finney.

A Journal Through Pregnancy

> My brain is practicing! It is sending
> brain waves to my eyes and ears!

Day 141   Date: _____

Think about your life fifteen years from now. What do you see?

_____
_____
_____
_____
_____
_____
_____
_____
_____
_____
_____
_____
_____

Daily Takeaway: *"Of course there is no formula for success except perhaps an unconditional acceptance of life and what it brings."* Arthur Rubenstein.

MAY I HAVE THIS DANCE?

> If I hear music, I can move to the rhythm!

Day 142   Date: _____

What fears did you have at the beginning of this pregnancy that no longer exist?

_____
_____
_____
_____
_____
_____
_____
_____
_____
_____
_____
_____

Daily Takeaway: *"Fear is the main source of superstition, and one of the main sources of cruelty. To conquer fear is the beginning of wisdom."* Bertrand Russell.

A Journal Through Pregnancy

> My eyelids are re-opening!

Day 143 Date: _____

What happened to make the fear(s) go away that you wrote of yesterday?

_____
_____
_____
_____
_____
_____
_____
_____
_____
_____
_____
_____

Daily Takeaway: *"Courage is fear that has said its prayers."* Dorothy Bernard.

> I'm two-thirds of the way done in here. Only three more months until I see you for the first time!

Day 144 Date: _____

Has anyone shared a horrific childbirth story with you? If so, what did you think about it?

_____

Daily Takeaway: *"Do not anticipate trouble, or worry about what may never happen. Keep in the sunlight."* Benjamin Franklin.

A Journal Through Pregnancy

> All my bones are here, but
> they're not all connected yet.

Day 145   Date: _____

What do you think your child will like the most about you?

_____
_____
_____
_____
_____
_____
_____
_____
_____
_____
_____
_____
_____

Daily Takeaway: *"Sometimes the laughter in mothering is the recognition of the ironies and absurdities. Sometimes, though, it's just pure, unthinking delight."* Barbara Schapiro.

MAY I HAVE THIS DANCE?

> I'm going to grow another
> half-inch this week. I'm getting so tall!

Day 146 Date: _____

What do you believe your child will like the least about you?

___

Daily Takeaway: *"A mother is not a person to lean on, but a person to make leaning unnecessary."* Dorothy Fisher.

A Journal Through Pregnancy

> My lungs and brain seem to have the most activity. WOW! There's a lot going on in here.

Day 147   Date: _____

What fun things do you want to do with your child?

_____
_____
_____
_____
_____
_____
_____
_____
_____
_____
_____
_____

Daily Takeaway: *"Our imagination is the only limit to what we can hope to have in the future."* Charles Kettering.

MAY I HAVE THIS DANCE?

> I'm getting really big. Is it getting hard for you to breathe? Sorry.

Day 148 Date: _____

How will you encourage your child to be who he/she wants to be?

___

Daily Takeaway: *"Go confidently in the direction of your dreams. Live the life you have imagined."* Henry David Thoreau.

A Journal Through Pregnancy

> If I wanted to cry, I could now!

Day 149 Date: _____

What are your thoughts and feelings about disciplining your child?

Daily Takeaway: *"Patience is the companion of wisdom."* Saint Augustine.

MAY I HAVE THIS DANCE?

> I'm around fourteen inches long!

Day 150 Date: _____

What is one way you can show your child your love?

_____
_____
_____
_____
_____
_____
_____
_____
_____
_____
_____
_____
_____

Daily Takeaway: *"To love and be loved is to feel the sun from both sides."* David Viscott.

A Journal Through Pregnancy

> Am I going to be tall or short? I hope I look like you!

Day 151   Date: _____

What in your life should you give up for your child, but are afraid to?

_____

_____

_____

_____

_____

_____

_____

_____

_____

_____

_____

_____

_____

Daily Takeaway: *"Fear is a question; what are you afraid of and why? Just as the seed of health is in illness, your fears are a treasure house of self-knowledge if you explore them."* Marilyn Ferguson.

> Mommy . . . I love you!

Day 152 Date: _____

What did you learn as a child that will help you raise your child?

___

Daily Takeaway: *"Knowledge is power."* Sir Francis Bacon.

A Journal Through Pregnancy

> Did you know when I'm asleep I sometimes dream?

Day 153   Date: _____

Name one personal issue you are working through during this pregnancy and write about it.

_____
_____
_____
_____
_____
_____
_____
_____
_____
_____
_____
_____
_____
_____

○━━▸━○

Daily Takeaway: *"We improve ourselves by victory over our self. There must be contests and you must win."* Edward Gibbons.

> I'm starting to store some fat under my wrinkly skin.

Day 154 Date: _____

How have your feelings changed from the day you found out you were pregnant?

_____
_____
_____
_____
_____
_____
_____
_____
_____
_____
_____
_____

Daily Takeaway: *"If you think you can win, you can win. Faith is necessary to victory."* William Hazlitt.

A Journal Through Pregnancy

> My eyes are completely formed. They might be blue when I'm born, but then they might stay blue or change colors.

Day 155 Date: _____

What traditions would you like to start with your child?

___

Daily Takeaway: *"The best way to predict the future is to invent it."* Alan Kay.

MAY I HAVE THIS DANCE?

> My swallowing skills are getting better.

Day 156 Date: _____

How have you been blessed during this pregnancy?

_____
_____
_____
_____
_____
_____
_____
_____
_____
_____
_____
_____

Daily Takeaway: *"The goodness of God is the drive behind all the blessings He daily bestows upon us."* A. W. Tozer.

A Journal Through Pregnancy

> My lungs are now fully capable of breathing air!

Day 157　　　　　　　　Date: _____

What is one thing in your life you need to change before you have your baby?

_____

_____

_____

_____

_____

_____

_____

_____

_____

_____

_____

_____

_____

_____

Daily Takeaway: *"Only I can change my life. No one can do it for me."* Carol Burnett.

MAY I HAVE THIS DANCE?

> I sure am warm and snugly in here!

Day 158   Date: _____

How do you plan to change what you wrote about yesterday?

_____
_____
_____
_____
_____
_____
_____
_____
_____
_____
_____
_____
_____

Daily Takeaway: *"Change your thoughts and you change your world."* Norman Vincent Peale.

A Journal Through Pregnancy

> Mommy . . . I love being this close to you!

Day 159 Date: _____

Take today off and rest your mind. Don't allow your mind to linger on any doubts, worries, or fears. Just rest.

_____
_____
_____
_____
_____
_____
_____
_____
_____
_____
_____

Daily Takeaway: *"Don't worry about anything. Instead, pray about everything. Tell God what you need, and thank Him for all He has done. If you do this, you will experience God's peace, which is far more wonderful than the human mind can understand. His peace will guard your heart and mind as you live in Christ Jesus."* Philippians 4:6-7 NLT.

MAY I HAVE THIS DANCE?

> I can see bright lights through your tummy!

Day 160 Date: _____

What is another way you can show your child your love?

_____
_____
_____
_____
_____
_____
_____
_____
_____
_____
_____
_____
_____

Daily Takeaway: *"Your children are a gift to you. How you raise them is your gift to the world."* Anonymous.

A Journal Through Pregnancy

> My ability to live outside
> your tummy is improving every day!

Day 161 Date: _____

What do you plan to do about working once your child is born?

___

Daily Takeaway: *"Every mother is a working mother."* Anonymous.

MAY I HAVE THIS DANCE?

> My skin is getting smoother because I'm getting fatter. Keep that good food coming!

Day 162 Date: _____

What is your dream job?

_____
_____
_____
_____
_____
_____
_____
_____
_____
_____
_____
_____
_____
_____

Daily Takeaway: *"Pleasure in the job puts perfection in the work."* Aristotle.

A Journal Through Pregnancy

> I'm practicing looking around.
> I like moving my eyes back and forth.

Day 163 Date: _____

What steps would you have to take to make your dream job become a reality? Go back to school? Move to a new city?

_____

_____

_____

_____

_____

_____

_____

_____

_____

_____

_____

_____

_____

Daily Takeaway: *"Real success is finding your life's work in the work that you love."* David McCullough.

MAY I HAVE THIS DANCE?

> If you have picked out my name, please say it often. I like hearing your voice say my name!

Day 164   Date: _____

What are the activities you have enjoyed the most during your pregnancy?

Daily Takeaway: *"What we nurture in ourselves will grow. This is nature's eternal law."* Johann Wolfgang von Goethe.

A Journal Through Pregnancy

> Do you have any clothes for me yet?
> I'm going to need lots of diapers!

Day 165 Date: _____

How can you include your baby in your favorite activities?

_____
_____
_____
_____
_____
_____
_____
_____
_____
_____
_____
_____

Daily Takeaway: *"To love deeply in one direction makes us more loving in all others."* Anne-Sophie Swetchine.

MAY I HAVE THIS DANCE?

> My nice little home is getting more cramped.
> I can't stretch my legs out any longer.

Day 166 Date: _____

What is one skill you would like to teach your child? Piano? Swimming?

_____
_____
_____
_____
_____
_____
_____
_____
_____
_____
_____
_____

Daily Takeaway: *"The whole art of teaching is only the art of awakening the natural curiosity of a young mind for the purpose of satisfying it afterwards."* Anatole France.

A Journal Through Pregnancy

> My toenails are almost fully formed!

Day 167 Date: _____

Do you enjoy reading? If so, what are some of your favorite books and/or authors, and why?

_____

_____

_____

_____

_____

_____

_____

_____

_____

_____

_____

_____

_____

Daily Takeaway: *"Books are the quietest and most constant friends; they are the most accessible and wisest of counselors, and the most patient of teachers."* Charles Eliot.

MAY I HAVE THIS DANCE?

> I'm really starting to fill out and grow into my skin!

Day 168 Date: _____

Write about the baby names you are thinking about and why you like them.

_____
_____
_____
_____
_____
_____
_____
_____
_____
_____
_____
_____
_____

Daily Takeaway: *"Babies are such a nice way to start people."* Don Herold.

A Journal Through Pregnancy

> I weigh about three pounds!

Day 169   Date: _____

What steps can you take to live in this moment, so fears of the future will not overwhelm you?

_____
_____
_____
_____
_____
_____
_____
_____
_____
_____
_____
_____
_____

Daily Takeaway: *"Never let the future disturb you. You will meet it with the same weapons of reason which today arm you against the present."* Marcus Aurelius.

MAY I HAVE THIS DANCE?

> My brain is getting wrinkly, meaning it's getting more powerful!

Day 170   Date: _____

What are your ideas for an ideal birth?

_____
_____
_____
_____
_____
_____
_____
_____
_____
_____

Daily Takeaway: *"Birthing is the liberation of the child from the dark prison of the womb into the light. The one who is sealed is being discharged. But relief comes for the mother, too, with release of the tremendously heavy burden from her belly and sweet, sweet reprieve from pain. It is over. The job is done! The blessed cord that binds is broken, and a better, stronger tie of love between Mother and baby is created."* **Nine Months and Counting**, Alice Chapin.

A Journal Through Pregnancy

> I'm starting to store the nutrients you're sending me!

Day 171   Date: _____

What is another way you can show your child your love?

_____
_____
_____
_____
_____
_____
_____
_____
_____
_____
_____
_____

Daily Takeaway: *"Love is everything it's cracked up to be. . . . It really is worth fighting for, being brave for, risking everything for."* Erica Jong.

MAY I HAVE THIS DANCE?

> I'm beginning to press against your ribs.
> I hope I'm not making you too uncomfortable!

Day 172   Date: _____

How do you feel about your growing belly?

_____
_____
_____
_____
_____
_____
_____
_____
_____
_____
_____
_____

Daily Takeaway: *"I feel like a cow; I haven't gotten angry in weeks. I am happy and contented. That satisfied smile must be driving some of my friends crazy with envy, or at least I hope it is. For the first time in my life, I have an excuse for being plump."*
Angela Barron McBride.

A Journal Through Pregnancy

> My whole body was covered by hair, but now most of that is gone. I'm getting ready to come and see you!

Day 173 Date: _____

How much weight have you gained during your pregnancy?

_____
_____
_____
_____
_____
_____
_____
_____
_____
_____
_____

Daily Takeaway: *"Remember to take frequent stress breaks during a busy day. Take a few minutes for prayer, for exercise, for hydration, and to regain perspective."*
101 **Ways to Relax and Reduce Stress**, Candy Paull.

MAY I HAVE THIS DANCE?

> I'm going to gain another pound this month!

Day 174 Date: _____

How do you feel about using anesthesia during childbirth?

_____
_____
_____
_____
_____
_____
_____
_____
_____
_____
_____
_____

Daily Takeaway: *"I know the Lord is always with me. I will not be shaken for He is right beside me. . . . My body rests in hope."* Acts 2:25-26 NLT.

A Journal Through Pregnancy

> Did you know that when I hear your voice my heart beats faster?

Day 175   Date: _____

How have your emotions changed since becoming pregnant?

_____

_____

_____

_____

_____

_____

_____

_____

_____

_____

_____

Daily Takeaway: *"Each of us makes our own weather, and determines the color of the skies in the emotional universe which he inhabits."* Fulton Sheen.

MAY I HAVE THIS DANCE?

> My growth is slowing down a little bit.

Day 176 Date: _____

What are two surprising changes in your body?

_____

_____

_____

_____

_____

_____

_____

_____

_____

_____

_____

_____

_____

_____

Daily Takeaway: *"Each body has its art."* Gwendolyn Brooks.

A Journal Through Pregnancy

> I might have a callous on my thumb when I'm born because I've been sucking it so much!

Day 177 Date: _____

What part of motherhood do you think you will like the most?

Daily Takeaway: *"The art of mothering is to teach the art of living to children."* Elain Heffner.

MAY I HAVE THIS DANCE?

> Even though I have some of your blood in my veins, I have my own unique separate supply.

Day 178 Date: _____

What part of motherhood do you think you will like the least?

Daily Takeaway: *"The most important thing she'd learned over the years was that there was no way to be a perfect mother and a million ways to be a good one."* Jill Churchill.

A Journal Through Pregnancy

> God is working overtime to develop my brain!

Day 179 Date: _____

Take today off and rest your mind. Don't allow your mind to linger on any doubts, worries, or fears. Just rest.

_____

_____

_____

_____

_____

_____

_____

_____

_____

_____

_____

○―✦―○

Daily Takeaway: *"Don't worry about anything. Instead, pray about everything. Tell God what you need, and thank Him for all He has done. If you do this you will experience God's peace, which is far more wonderful than the human mind can understand. His peace will guard your heart and mind as you live in Christ Jesus."* Philippians 4:6-7 NLT.

MAY I HAVE THIS DANCE?

> I'm craving milk. Please drink lots and lots of it.

Day 180   Date: _____

What do you know about the hospital you will be using?

_____
_____
_____
_____
_____
_____
_____
_____
_____
_____
_____

Daily Takeaway: *"By focusing on one task or goal at a time, you harness the full energy of your mind. Being focused helps you accomplish more in the long run."*
101 **Ways to Relax and Reduce Stress**, Candy Paull.

A Journal Through Pregnancy

> All five of my senses are now working!

Day 181 Date: _____

Think about your life twenty years from now. What do you see?

Daily Takeaway: *"To accomplish great things, we must dream as well as act."* Anatole France.

MAY I HAVE THIS DANCE?

> Sometimes everything in here gets real small and tight. Are you having practice contractions?

Day 182 Date: _____

What do you think your baby is going to look like?

_____
_____
_____
_____
_____
_____
_____
_____
_____
_____
_____
_____
_____

Daily Takeaway: *"Who is best taught? He who first learned from his mother."* The Talmud.

A Journal Through Pregnancy

> I hope you're not too uncomfortable. It won't be long now!

Day 183   Date: _____

Do you think your child will play sports? If so, which ones?

_____

_____

_____

_____

_____

_____

_____

_____

_____

_____

_____

_____

Daily Takeaway: *"Sports serve society by providing vivid examples of excellence."* George Will.

> Mommy . . . I love you more
> and more with each passing day!

Day 184   Date: _____

What has been the best part of being pregnant?

_____
_____
_____
_____
_____
_____
_____
_____
_____
_____
_____
_____

Daily Takeaway: *"And I pray that Christ will be more and more at home in your hearts as you trust in him. May your roots go down deep into the soil of God's marvelous love."* Ephesians 3:17 NLT.

A Journal Through Pregnancy

> There is almost no space left in here!

Day 185 Date: _____

What has been the worst part of being pregnant?

_____
_____
_____
_____
_____
_____
_____
_____
_____
_____
_____
_____

Daily Takeaway: *"And may you have the power to understand, as all God's people should, how wide, how long, how high, and how deep his love really is. May you experience the love of Christ, though it is so great you will never fully understand it. Then you will be filled with the fullness of life and power that comes from God."* Ephesians 3:18-19 NLT.

MAY I HAVE THIS DANCE?

> I hope you're not getting nervous about my arrival. We're going to make a great team!

Day 186 Date: _____

As you get closer to being a mother, what thoughts are you having about your own mother?

_____
_____
_____
_____
_____
_____
_____
_____
_____
_____
_____
_____
_____

Daily Takeaway: *"My mother had a great deal of trouble with me, but I think she enjoyed it."* Mark Twain.

A Journal Through Pregnancy

> I'm an inch longer than I was four days ago!

Day 187 Date: _____

How have you learned patience during this pregnancy?

_____
_____
_____
_____
_____
_____
_____
_____
_____
_____
_____
_____
_____

Daily Takeaway: *"So let it grow, for when your patience is fully developed, you will be strong in character and ready for anything."* James 1:4 NLT.

MAY I HAVE THIS DANCE?

> It doesn't matter if my skin is
> light or dark. Right now, it's pink!

Day 188   Date: _____

Has anyone said anything hurtful to you? If so, how did it make you feel?

_____

_____

_____

_____

_____

_____

_____

_____

_____

_____

_____

Daily Takeaway: *"Don't mind criticism. If it's untrue, disregard it; if it's unfair, keep from irritation; if it's ignorant, smile; if it's justified, learn from it."* Anonymous.

A Journal Through Pregnancy

> I have more and more fat
> being produced under my skin!

Day 189   Date: _____

Regarding what you wrote about yesterday, what is the truth regarding those hurtful comments?

_____
_____
_____
_____
_____
_____
_____
_____
_____
_____
_____
_____
_____
_____

Daily Takeaway: *"When attacked by a dragon, do not become one."* Marshall Shelley.

> I'm moving around a whole lot less. I like to sleep a lot.

Day 190　　　　　Date: _____

What changes if any, have you experienced with your thought processes?

___

Daily Takeaway: *"Commit your works to the Lord, and your thoughts will be established."* Proverbs 16:3 **NKJV**.

A Journal Through Pregnancy

> I'm trying to turn so I'll be
> headed in the right direction!

Day 191 Date: _____

What is another way you can show your child your love?

_____

_____

_____

_____

_____

_____

_____

_____

_____

_____

_____

Daily Takeaway: *"Love is patient and kind. Love is not jealous or boastful or proud or rude. Love does not demand its own way. Love is not irritable, and it keeps no record of when it has been wronged. It is never glad about injustice but rejoices whenever the truth wins out. Love never gives up, never loses faith, is always hopeful, and endures through every circumstance."* I Corinthians 13:4-7 NLT.

MAY I HAVE THIS DANCE?

> My lungs are putting on the finishing touches!

Day 192 Date: _____

What are some childhood games you will teach your child?

_____

_____

_____

_____

_____

_____

_____

_____

_____

_____

_____

_____

_____

_____

Daily Takeaway: *"Good teaching is one-fourth preparation and three-fourths theater."* Gail Godwin.

A Journal Through Pregnancy

> I'm almost completely ready to see you!

Day 193   Date: _____

What is a major fear you are having at this point in your pregnancy?

_____
_____
_____
_____
_____
_____
_____
_____
_____
_____
_____
_____
_____

○—✦—○

Daily Takeaway: *"Do not pray for easy lives. Pray to be stronger men! Do not pray for tasks equal to your powers. Pray for powers equal to your tasks!"* Phillips Brooks.

MAY I HAVE THIS DANCE?

> This week my fingernails
> are going to reach my fingertips!

Day 194 Date: _____

Who is someone you can trust to talk with about the fear you wrote of yesterday? Why do you trust him/her? Talk to them today about this fear.

_____
_____
_____
_____
_____
_____
_____
_____
_____
_____
_____
_____

Daily Takeaway: *"You may be deceived if you trust too much, but you will live in torment if you do not trust enough."* Frank Crane.

A Journal Through Pregnancy

> If I were born this week, I would probably be fine.

Day 195 Date: _____

Write about the conversation you had yesterday.

_____
_____
_____
_____
_____
_____
_____
_____
_____
_____
_____
_____

○━━○

Daily Takeaway: *"When you really trust someone, you have to be okay with not understanding some things."*
Real Live Preacher—real live preacher web log, July 8, 2004.

MAY I HAVE THIS DANCE?

> WOW! My brain is still growing very quickly.

Day 196 Date: _____

What strange or exciting dreams have you had lately?

_____
_____
_____
_____
_____
_____
_____
_____
_____
_____
_____
_____
_____

○─✦─○

Daily Takeaway: *"Dreaming permits each and every one of us to be quietly and safely insane every night of our lives."* William Dement.

A Journal Through Pregnancy

> My skin is becoming very smooth and soft.

Day 197   Date: _____

Explain your nursery, or what you want to do with your nursery.

_____
_____
_____
_____
_____
_____
_____
_____
_____
_____
_____
_____
_____

Daily Takeaway: *"A good home must be made, not bought."* Joyce Maynard.

MAY I HAVE THIS DANCE?

> OUCH! I just scratched myself!

Day 198 Date: _____

Has anyone gotten you a gift yet? Explain.

_____
_____
_____
_____
_____
_____
_____
_____
_____
_____
_____
_____

Daily Takeaway: *"Every good thing given and every perfect gift is from above, coming down from the Father of lights, with whom there is no variation or shifting shadow."* James 1:17 NASB.

A Journal Through Pregnancy

> If I were to keep growing at this rate once I'm born, I would weight 200 pounds on my first birthday!

Day 199   Date: _____

Take today off and rest your mind. Don't allow your mind to linger on any doubts, worries, or fears. Just rest.

___

Daily Takeaway: *"Don't worry about anything. Instead, pray about everything. Tell God what you need, and thank Him for all He has done. If you do this you will experience God's peace, which is far more wonderful than the human mind can understand. His peace will guard your heart and mind as you live in Christ Jesus."* Philippians 4:6-7 NLT.

MAY I HAVE THIS DANCE?

> My belly has become really round!

Day 200 Date: _____

What is it about childbirth that excites you the most?

_____
_____
_____
_____
_____
_____
_____
_____
_____
_____
_____
_____
_____

Daily Takeaway: *"I wait quietly upon God, for my hope is in Him."* Psalms 62:5 NLT.

A Journal Through Pregnancy

> I'm trying to get situated
> in here so I'll come out easier!

Day 201 Date: _____

What is another way you can show your love to your child?

_____

_____

_____

_____

_____

_____

_____

_____

_____

_____

_____

_____

_____

Daily Takeaway: *"What a child doesn't receive, he can seldom later give."* P. D. James.

MAY I HAVE THIS DANCE?

> Mommy . . . I'm so excited to see you!

Day 202 Date: _____

How can you make your home safer for your child?

_____
_____
_____
_____
_____
_____
_____
_____
_____
_____
_____

Daily Takeaway: *"Dear friend, I am praying that all is well with you and that your body is as healthy as I know your soul is."*
III John 1:2 NLT.

A Journal Through Pregnancy

> My arms are looking chubby!

Day 203　　　　　　Date: _____

Who do you want with you during the childbirth? Why?

_____
_____
_____
_____
_____
_____
_____
_____
_____
_____
_____
_____
_____

Daily Takeaway: *"Jesus was not above being a servant. Be like Him and honor others with simple kindness today. It will warm your heart, too."* 101 Ways to Relax and Reduce Stress, Candy Paull.

MAY I HAVE THIS DANCE?

> Sometimes my foot gets caught under your ribs. Sorry about that!

Day 204   Date: _____

What will be the first major holiday you celebrate with your child? How can you make it special?

_____
_____
_____
_____
_____
_____
_____
_____
_____
_____
_____
_____
_____

Daily Takeaway: *"Outings are so much more fun when we can savor them through the children's eyes."* Lawana Blackwell.

A Journal Through Pregnancy

> I'm over a foot long!

Day 205   Date: _____

How do you picture God?

_____
_____
_____
_____
_____
_____
_____
_____
_____
_____
_____

Daily Takeaway: *"God is a spirit, infinite, eternal, and unchangeable in His being, wisdom, power, holiness, justice, goodness, and truth."* Answer to the fourth question of the **Westminster Shorter Catechism**, a statement that theologian Charles Hodge described as *"probably the best definition of God ever penned by man."*

MAY I HAVE THIS DANCE?

> I've been storing nutrients for a while, just in case I'm born early!

Day 206 Date: _____

Do you feel that yesterday's portrayal of God is accurate? Why or why not?

_____

_____

_____

_____

_____

_____

_____

_____

_____

_____

_____

_____

_____

Daily Takeaway: *"Disregard the study of God, and you sentence yourself to stumble and blunder through life blindfolded, as it were, with no sense of direction."* J. I. Packer.

A Journal Through Pregnancy

> It won't be long now.
> We're on the homestretch, Mommy!

Day 207   Date: _____

What does the word "character" mean to you?

_____

_____

_____

_____

_____

_____

_____

_____

_____

_____

_____

_____

Daily Takeaway: *"People grow through experience if they meet life honestly and courageously. This is how character is built."*
Eleanor Roosevelt.

MAY I HAVE THIS DANCE?

> This cord has done a lot of the work for me, so my gastrointestinal system won't fully function for several years.

Day 208   Date: _____

Describe what you believe about God's character.

_____
_____
_____
_____
_____
_____
_____
_____
_____
_____
_____
_____
_____

Daily Takeaway: *"With the goodness of God to desire our highest welfare, the wisdom of God to plan it, and the power of God to achieve it, what do we lack?"* A. W. Tozer.

A Journal Through Pregnancy

> All this fat that's going under my
> skin is helping to maintain my temperature.

Day 209 Date: _____

Write about someone you know, someone you believe has good character.

___

Daily Takeaway: *"Personality can open doors, but only character can keep them open."* Elmer Letterman.

MAY I HAVE THIS DANCE?

> My growth has slowed down a bit.
> I'm conserving my energy for childbirth.

Day 210   Date: _____

Describe how you want your baby's character to be.

_____
_____
_____
_____
_____
_____
_____
_____
_____
_____
_____
_____
_____

Daily Takeaway: *"Forming characters! Whose? Our own or others? Both. And in that momentous fact lies the peril and the responsibility of our existence."* Elihu Burritt.

A Journal Through Pregnancy

> I have dimples in my elbows!

Day 211   Date: _____

Do you believe God changes His mind? Why or why not?

_____
_____
_____
_____
_____
_____
_____
_____
_____
_____
_____
_____

Daily Takeaway: *"God never changes moods or cools off in His affections or loses enthusiasm."* A. W. Tozer.

MAY I HAVE THIS DANCE?

> I have dimples in my knees!

Day 212 Date: _____

Is God active in your life? Why or why not?

_____
_____
_____
_____
_____
_____
_____
_____
_____
_____
_____
_____
_____

Daily Takeaway: *". . . I will never fail you, I will never forsake you."* Hebrews 13:5 NLT.

A Journal Through Pregnancy

> My gums look like teeth are about to break through, but that won't happen for some time.

Day 213 Date: _____

Is there something you need that you believe God can't provide? If so, what is that need?

_____

_____

_____

_____

_____

_____

_____

_____

_____

_____

_____

_____

Daily Takeaway: *"This I declare of the LORD: He alone is my refuge, my place of safety; He is my God, and I am trusting him."* Psalm 91:2 NLT.

MAY I HAVE THIS DANCE?

> I recognize the familiar voices around you!

Day 214 Date: _____

How does it make you feel to know that God is walking through this pregnancy with you?

___

Daily Takeaway: *"Be strong and of a good courage, fear not, nor be afraid of them: for the LORD thy God, He [it is] that doth go with thee; He will not fail thee, nor forsake thee."* Deuteronomy 31:6 NLT.

A Journal Through Pregnancy

> I get the hiccups a lot. Do you feel them, too?

Day 215 Date: _____

Does it calm you or make you uneasy to think God is close to you?

_____

_____

_____

_____

_____

_____

_____

_____

_____

_____

_____

_____

Daily Takeaway: *"God showed me He had been with me every day of my life, through every experience past and present. He showed me He even existed where no man or woman including myself could ever go. He was in my tomorrows."* Angela Klinger.

MAY I HAVE THIS DANCE?

> My grip has gotten a lot stronger!

Day 216 Date: _____

How do you feel every time you hear the baby's heartbeat?

_____

_____

_____

_____

_____

_____

_____

_____

_____

_____

_____

_____

Daily Takeaway: *"There is a new life growing inside that is nearly perfected. A new human being will soon come forth. The Lord has done glorious things!"* **Nine Months and Counting**, Alice Chapin.

A Journal Through Pregnancy

> Not all of my cartilage has turned to bone, making it easier for me to come out!

Day 217   Date: _____

Explain what you believe the childbirth experience will be like.

_____
_____
_____
_____
_____
_____
_____
_____
_____
_____
_____
_____

Daily Takeaway: *"Love which bubbled underground for forty weeks, bursts skyward in a geyser and melts heaven's gates. In one eternal moment I hear angel choirs echo my alleluias to your maker and mine."*
Loving Your Preborn Baby, Carol Van Klompenburg.

MAY I HAVE THIS DANCE?

> I can see really well. When a light
> is turned on, I automatically turn toward it.

Day 218 Date: _____

Are you able to be flexible if childbirth doesn't go as planned?

_____
_____
_____
_____
_____
_____
_____
_____
_____
_____
_____

Daily Takeaway: *"I am still determined to be cheerful and happy in whatever situation I may be; for I have also learned from experience that greater part of our happiness or misery depends upon our dispositions, and not upon our circumstances."* Martha Washington.

A Journal Through Pregnancy

> My toenails have reached the end of my toes. You might need to clip them as soon as I'm born.

Day 219 Date: _____

Take today off and rest your mind. Don't allow your mind to linger on any doubts, worries, or fears. Just rest.

_____

_____

_____

_____

_____

_____

_____

_____

_____

_____

Daily Takeaway: *"Don't worry about anything. Instead, pray about everything. Tell God what you need, and thank Him for all He has done. If you do this you will experience God's peace, which is far more wonderful than the human mind can understand. His peace will guard your heart and mind as you live in Christ Jesus."* Philippians 4:6-7 NLT.

MAY I HAVE THIS DANCE?

> I can tell it's almost time to leave my nice, warm home!

Day 220 Date: _____

Write out some of the comments made by your doctor or midwife and people you know that have made you feel good.

_____
_____
_____
_____
_____
_____
_____
_____
_____
_____
_____
_____
_____

Daily Takeaway: *"Many of our daily conversations are actually mutual counseling sessions whereby we exchange the reassurance and advice that help us deal with routine stresses."* National Institute of Mental Health.

A Journal Through Pregnancy

> God is now starting my final touches!

Day 221　　　　　　Date: _____

What are some of the physical challenges you are having at this point in your pregnancy?

_____

_____

_____

_____

_____

_____

_____

_____

_____

_____

_____

_____

Daily Takeaway: *"Lord, sometimes it seems all that I am is my bulging belly. It is what everybody sees and talks about when we meet. I am defined as pregnant. It helps to remind myself often that I am much more than a mother-to-be. I am a person with talents, abilities, hopes, ambitions, fears, longings, and passions."* **Book of Common Prayer.**

MAY I HAVE THIS DANCE?

> I have my own immune system!

Day 222   Date: _____

As the birth approaches, what are you most excited about?

_____
_____
_____
_____
_____
_____
_____
_____
_____
_____
_____
_____

Daily Takeaway: *"God speaks to all individuals through what happens to them moment by moment."* J. P. DeCaussade.

A Journal Through Pregnancy

> Your blood has supplied me with antibodies!

Day 223 Date: _____

As the birth approaches, do you have any new fears or apprehensions?

Daily Takeaway: *"Fear is the main source of superstition, and one of the main sources of cruelty. To conquer fear is the beginning of wisdom."* Bertrand Russell.

MAY I HAVE THIS DANCE?

> I'm going to gain two more pounds this month!

Day 224　　　　　Date: _____

How is your family reacting to the upcoming addition of this child?

___

Daily Takeaway: *"Do you call life a bad job? Never! We've had our ups and downs, we've had our struggles, we've always been poor, but it's been worth it, worth it a hundred times I say when I look round at my children."* W. Somerset Maugham.

A Journal Through Pregnancy

> Even though my growth has slowed, fat deposits are being made under my skin every day!

Day 225　　　　　Date: _____

What are the things you need to take care of before the baby arrives?

_____
_____
_____
_____
_____
_____
_____
_____
_____
_____
_____
_____
_____

Daily Takeaway: *"No job can compete with the responsibility of shaping and molding a new human being."* Dr. James Dobson.

MAY I HAVE THIS DANCE?

> My muscles have grown very strong!

Day 226 Date: _____

What has been most special about this time in your life?

_____
_____
_____
_____
_____
_____
_____
_____
_____
_____
_____

Daily Takeaway: *"Having a child is not an unbearable responsibility, but an opportunity to shape a little child's future. You are privileged to get to calm the baby's fears and nurture him as he grows. You will have the most impact on this child's life and in return . . . love unconditional."* 29-year-old mom when asked, *"What advice would you give a mother-to-be?"*

A Journal Through Pregnancy

> All my organs are almost completely developed!

Day 227 Date: _____

What have you enjoyed the most about being pregnant?

_____
_____
_____
_____
_____
_____
_____
_____
_____
_____

Daily Takeaway: *"Therefore, since we are surrounded by such a huge crowd of witnesses to the life of faith, let us strip off every weight that slows us down, especially the sin that so easily hinders our progress. And let us run with endurance the race that God has set before us. We do this by keeping our eyes on Jesus, on whom our faith depends from start to finish. He was willing to die a shameful death on the cross because of the joy he knew would be his afterward. Now he is seated in the place of highest honor beside God's throne in heaven."* Hebrews 12:1-2 NLT.

MAY I HAVE THIS DANCE?

> My lungs still need a little time, but I would probably be fine if I were born today!

Day 228   Date: _____

Who are the people in your life who are supporting you the most?

_____

_____

_____

_____

_____

_____

_____

_____

_____

_____

_____

Daily Takeaway: *"Do not protect yourself by a fence, but rather by your friends."* Czech Proverb.

A Journal Through Pregnancy

> Mommy . . . I hope I look like you.

Day 229 Date: _____

What do you have left to do to prepare your baby's nursery?

_____
_____
_____
_____
_____
_____
_____
_____
_____
_____
_____

Daily Takeaway: *"Doing creative projects — putting paint on canvas, shaping clay, knitting, weaving, gardening, wood-working — renews your soul and gives you a welcome respite from the stress of the workaday world."* 101 Ways to Relax and Reduce Stress, Candy Paull.

MAY I HAVE THIS DANCE?

> Please don't be nervous about my arrival.
> We have a long time to get to know each other!

Day 230 Date: _____

What do you believe life will be like after your baby is born?

_____
_____
_____
_____
_____
_____
_____
_____
_____
_____
_____

Daily Takeaway: *Ask a mother you know if what you wrote about today is realistic.*

A Journal Through Pregnancy

> My skin is getting thicker
> and turning the color of yours!

Day 231　　　　　Date: _____

Write about what the mother you spoke to explained.

_____
_____
_____
_____
_____
_____
_____
_____
_____
_____
_____
_____
_____

Daily Takeaway: *"Advice – Helping another with one's own wisdom. Wisdom – True and tested facts learned through life experience."*
Sheila Harper.

MAY I HAVE THIS DANCE?

> I'm gaining about a half an ounce a day now!

Day 232   Date: _____

How will you deal with not getting as much sleep as you're accustomed to?

_____
_____
_____
_____
_____
_____
_____
_____
_____
_____
_____
_____

Daily Takeaway: *"People who say they sleep like a baby usually don't have one."* Leo Burke.

A Journal Through Pregnancy

> When you see me cry, I probably won't have tears. My tear ducts will be ready in a couple of weeks.

Day 233 Date: _____

How do you feel about this weight gain?

_____
_____
_____
_____
_____
_____
_____
_____
_____
_____
_____
_____

Daily Takeaway: *"Be still and cool in thy own mind and spirit."* George Fox.

MAY I HAVE THIS DANCE?

> This umbilical cord is really long. You're going to be surprised!

Day 234 Date: _____

How much weight have I gained? What is my plan for losing the additional pounds after childbirth?

_____
_____
_____
_____
_____
_____
_____
_____
_____
_____
_____
_____

Daily Takeaway: *"God gives us always strength enough and sense enough for everything He wants us to do."* John Ruskin.

A Journal Through Pregnancy

> I can respond to sounds, light, and touch!

Day 235   Date: _____

What is the one activity with your child that you are looking forward to the most?

_____

_____

_____

_____

_____

_____

_____

_____

_____

_____

_____

Daily Takeaway: *"Experts say you will not spoil your new baby with a lot of holding. Newborns are not yet wise enough to try to control what you do. So plan to cuddle and hug whenever you can."*
Nine Months and Counting, Alice Chapin.

MAY I HAVE THIS DANCE?

> I know the difference between light
> and dark. I'm already getting so smart!

Day 236 Date: _____

What is the one downfall of our society that you want to shield your child from the most?

_____
_____
_____
_____
_____
_____
_____
_____
_____
_____
_____
_____
_____
_____

Daily Takeaway: *"To know the will of God is the greatest knowledge. To do the will of God is the greatest achievement."* George Truett.

A Journal Through Pregnancy

> The five pieces of my skull won't be
> stuck together until after I come out.
> That will make it easier for my head to come through!

Day 237 Date: _____

Explain how you will feel the first time you see your baby.

_____

_____

_____

_____

_____

_____

_____

_____

_____

_____

_____

_____

_____

_____

Daily Takeaway: *"Come behold the works of the Lord . . ."* Psalm 46:8.

MAY I HAVE THIS DANCE?

> Don't be alarmed if my head has
> an odd shape the first time you
> see me. It will straighten out in a few days.

Day 238   Date: _____

Write about your feelings on unconditional love.

_____

_____

_____

_____

_____

_____

_____

_____

_____

_____

_____

_____

Daily Takeaway: "During the first six months, the baby has the rudiments of a love language available to him. There is the language of the embrace, the language of the eyes, the language of the smile, and vocal communications of pleasure and distress. It is the essential vocabulary of love before he can speak." Selma Fraiber.

A Journal Through Pregnancy

> My chest is really filling out!

Day 239 Date: _____

Take today off and rest your mind. Don't allow your mind to linger on any doubts, worries, or fears. Just rest.

Daily Takeaway: *"Don't worry about anything. Instead, pray about everything. Tell God what you need, and thank Him for all He has done. If you do this, you will experience God's peace, which is far more wonderful than the human mind can understand. His peace will guard your heart and mind as you live in Christ Jesus."* Philippians 4:6-7 NLT.

MAY I HAVE THIS DANCE?

> I'm ready to see you!

Day 240 Date: _____

Do you believe your child will love you unconditionally? Why or why not?

_____
_____
_____
_____
_____
_____
_____
_____
_____
_____
_____
_____
_____
_____

Daily Takeaway: *"And the most important piece of clothing you must wear is love. Love is what binds us all together in perfect harmony."* Colossians 3:14 NLT.

A Journal Through Pregnancy

> Mommy, please don't be
> nervous; we're going to be fine!

Day 241 Date: _____

What is your plan to handle the pain associated with childbirth?

_____

_____

_____

_____

_____

_____

_____

_____

_____

_____

_____

_____

_____

Daily Takeaway: *"Lord, this is all so incredibly difficult! I do not deliver this baby alone. You know all about uneasy birthings. You are the perfect partner in my labor."* **Nine Months and Counting**, Alice Chapin.

MAY I HAVE THIS DANCE?

> I'm a fully functioning human being!

Day 242 Date: _____

Who do you want surrounding you during childbirth and in the days that follow?

Daily Takeaway: *"The world offers plenty of negative comments and criticism. You don't need more criticism. You need encouragement and support. A circle of supportive friends can encourage you to reach your full potential and make life easier and more fun."*
101 Ways to Relax and Reduce Stress, Candy Paull.

A Journal Through Pregnancy

> Thank you, Mommy, for carrying
> me these first nine months of my life!

Day 243 Date: _____

How do you feel physically? Explain.

_____
_____
_____
_____
_____
_____
_____
_____
_____
_____
_____
_____

Daily Takeaway: *"I finally realized that being grateful to my body was key to giving more love to myself."* Oprah Winfrey.

MAY I HAVE THIS DANCE?

> I really love it in here, but, boy, am I cramped!

Day 244 Date: _____

Where is your favorite place? The beach? The mountains? Explain.

Daily Takeaway: *Close your eyes, lean back in your chair, and allow yourself to visit your favorite place in your mind.*

A Journal Through Pregnancy

> I'm coming out any day now!

Day 245 Date: _____

How do you feel when you think about the moment you will realize you're in labor?

_____
_____
_____
_____
_____
_____
_____
_____
_____
_____
_____
_____
_____

Daily Takeaway: *"For myself I am an optimist — it doesn't seem to be much use being anything else."* Winston Churchill.

MAY I HAVE THIS DANCE?

> I hope you're as excited to see me as I am to see you!

Day 246 Date: _____

Think through the labor experience. How will you keep yourself from panicking?

_____
_____
_____
_____
_____
_____
_____
_____
_____
_____
_____
_____
_____

Daily Takeaway: *"God has not promised an easy way, but peace at the center of the hard way."*
Dale Evans.

A Journal Through Pregnancy

> Mommy . . . I love you!

Day 247   Date: _____

What are you most looking forward to regarding the labor and childbirth experience?

_____
_____
_____
_____
_____
_____
_____
_____
_____
_____
_____
_____

Daily Takeaway: *"The rush of waters when the amniotic sac breaks helps float the cargo of the precious newborn safely into the world. Lord, what marvelous planning! You are an awesome God!"*
Nine Months and Counting, Alice Chapin.

MAY I HAVE THIS DANCE?

> Mommy . . . I can't wait to feel you!

Day 248　　　　　　　Date: _____

Write out a prayer to God to watch over every portion of the labor and childbirth process.

_____
_____
_____
_____
_____
_____
_____
_____
_____
_____
_____
_____
_____
_____

Daily Takeaway: *"Prayer delights God's ear. It melts His heart, and it opens His hand. God cannot deny a praying soul."*
Thomas Watson.

A Journal Through Pregnancy

HERE I COME!

Day 249   Date: _____

Write down your true uninhibited feelings, fears, excitements, and anticipations. Get it all out on paper.

_____
_____
_____
_____
_____
_____
_____
_____
_____
_____

Daily Takeaway: *Pray like this: "Our Father in heaven, may your name be honored, may your Kingdom come soon. May your will be done here on earth, just as it is in heaven. Give us our food for today, and forgive us our sins, just as we have forgiven those who have sinned against us. And don't let us yield to temptation, but deliver us from the evil one. For yours is the kingdom and the power and the glory forever. Amen."* Matthew 6:9-13 NLT.

MAY I HAVE THIS DANCE?

A Journal Through Pregnancy

MAY I HAVE THIS DANCE?

A Journal Through Pregnancy

MAY I HAVE THIS DANCE?

A Journal Through Pregnancy

MAY I HAVE THIS DANCE?

A Journal Through Pregnancy

MAY I HAVE THIS DANCE?